JOURNAL FOR THE STUDY OF THE OLD TESTAMENT
SUPPLEMENT SERIES
127

Editors
David J.A. Clines
Philip R. Davies

JSOT Press
Sheffield

THE FABRIC OF HISTORY
Text, Artifact and Israel's Past

Edited by
Diana Vikander Edelman

Journal for the Study of the Old Testament
Supplement Series 127

Published by JSOT Press
JSOT Press is an imprint of
Sheffield Academic Press Ltd
The University of Sheffield
343 Fulwood Road
Sheffield S10 3BP
England

Typeset by Sheffield Academic Press
and
Printed on acid-free paper in Great Britain
by Billing & Sons Ltd
Worcester

A Catalogue record for this book is available from
the British Library

ISSN 0309-0787
ISBN 1-85075-324-5

CONTENTS

PREFACE

The essays in this volume were presented either *in toto* or in summary form at the 1989 Annual Society of Biblical Literature/American Schools of Oriental Research meeting in a symposium entitled 'The Role of History and Archaeology in Biblical Studies'. The papers by Gösta Ahlström, Max Miller and William Dever were intended to demonstrate how two historians and one archaeologist approach the task of historical reconstruction; how they interrelate textual and artifactual source materials that provide traces of past events within ancient Israel and Judah to create a reconstruction of the past. Both the disciplines of history and new archaeology are committed to the reconstruction of the past through its tangible remains.

Within biblical studies, historians tend to be most fully trained in the analysis of literary remains, while archaeologists tend to be most fully trained in the analysis of artifactual materials. Since the final goal of both groups is to provide a cogent interpretational framework that interrelates as much of the available textual and artifactual evidence as possible, in theory the general steps that need to be taken to accomplish a historical reconstruction should be shared by all three writers. This is true in spite of potential disagreements over the evaluation of particular evidence and the weight it should be given. Historians and archaeologists alike are often required to engage in the difficult task of evaluating the reliability and appropriateness of both text and artifact when undertaking their historical investigation. In many instances, they must rely upon the judgment of specialists in fields outside their own areas of expertise to make an informed evaluation about a given piece of potential evidence. Competence in historical reconstruction requires investigators to know and to accept their personal limitations. In addition, they must be willing to work with others outside their own fields and must know enough about the theories and *practica* of other disciplines to be able to judge whether the advice or evaluations of those turned to for assistance is generally trustworthy and representative of methods used within the field in question.

By printing their final essays side by side, it is hoped that a certain consensus can be found among the approaches espoused by the three. If there is not, then the reader can use the essays to judge where a lack of theoretical precision lies and to evaluate the relative strengths and weaknesses of each scholar's approach.

The essays by Axel Knauf and Thomas Thompson were designed to explore in a broad way two issues: (1) the relationship between historical research, historiography, and the Bible, and (2) the impact of new trends in the literary study of the Bible on historical research that uses the Bible as a source of evidence. The essay written by myself was meant to serve as a general summary of the boundaries of historical investigation within the discipline of biblical studies, which also touched upon the relationship of historical reconstruction to newly fashionable investigations conducted within the framework of social scientific disciplines. Having asked a number of colleagues to write this essay and having been turned down flatly, I was forced to undertake the task myself, as organizer of the symposium.

Clearly, the topic and issues addressed in these six essays are not new, and some may feel that enough ink has been wasted on such theoretical debates and discussions already. I would counter that not enough critical reflection has been done within our field about the nature of history and historical reconstruction and the place of history within biblical studies. The uncritical and often naïve use of both text and artifact that continues to dominate the majority of histories of Israel and Judah currently in print, including works that are used as standard references, resources and textbooks within our field, testifies to the need for a wider grassroots awareness of the basic issues involved in doing history as a biblical scholar. Although two main 'schools' associated with the names of Albrecht Alt and William Foxwell Albright continue to represent the bulk of historical research produced by those trained primarily as biblical scholars, a groundswell of dissatisfaction with both approaches can be detected among both American and continental scholars representing a variety of traditional backgrounds. A growing number are questioning the theoretical underpinnings of both schools and calling for or moving to an approach that makes a more critical evaluation of both textual and artifactual material before undertaking its use in historical reconstruction.

As we are in the midst of what can aptly be described metaphorically as the birth pains of a second child, it seems appropriate to re-examine the role of history and archaeology in biblical studies and to reopen discussion of issues raised by and related to the historical investigation of past events that transpired within ancient Israel and Judah. The present set of essays is offered in this spirit by a sampling of the ever-expanding group of scholars who are struggling with the redefinition of historical studies in the field of the Bible.

Diana Edelman
April, 1991

ABBREVIATIONS

AASOR	Annual of the American Schools of Oriental Research
ÄAT	Äegypten und Altes Testament
ADPV	Abhandlungen des Deutschen Palästina-Vereins
AJA	*American Journal of Archaeology*
ANET	*Ancient Near Eastern Texts* (ed. J.B. Pritchard; 3rd ed; Princeton: Princeton University, 1969).
AOAT	Alter Orient und Altes Testament
ATD	Das Alte Testament Deutsch
ATANT	Abhandlungen zur Theologie des Alten und Neuen Testaments
BA	*Biblical Archaeologist*
BARev	*Biblical Archaeology Review*
BASOR	*Bulletin of the American Schools of Oriental Research*
BETL	Bibliotheca ephemeridum theologicarum lovaniensium
Bib	*Biblica*
BN	*Biblische Notizen*
BTAVO	Beihefte zum *Tübinger Atlas der Vorderen Orients*
BWANT	Beiträge zur Wissenschaft vom Alten und Neuen Testament
BZAW	Beihefte zur *ZAW*
CBQMS	*Catholic Biblical Quarterly* Monograph Series
DBAT	*Dielheimer Blätter zum Alten Testament und seiner Rezeption in der Alte Kirche*
DMOA	Documenta et Monumenta Orientis Antiqui
EHST	Europäische Hochschulschriften Theologie
EI	*Eretz Israel*
FRLANT	Forschungen zur Religion und Literatur des Alten und Neuen Testaments
HSS	Harvard Semitic Studies
Int	*Interpretation*
JPOS	*Journal of the Palestine Oriental Society*
JSOT	*Journal for the Study of the Old Testament*
JSOTSup	*Journal for the Study of the Old Testament* Supplement Series
NKZ	*Neue kirchliche Zeitschrift*
OBO	Orbis biblicus et orientalis
OIP	Oriental Institute Publications
PEQ	*Palestine Exploration Quarterly*

PJ	*Palästina-Jahrbuch*
Phil-hist Kl	*Philologisch-historische Klasse*
R B	*Revue biblique*
SBLDS	SBL Dissertation Series
S BT	Studies in Biblical Theology
SBLMS	SBL Monograph Series
SBS	Stuttgarter Bibelstudien
SHANE	Studies in the History of the Ancient Near East
SWBAS	The Social World of Biblical Antiquity Series
TLZ	*Theologischer Literaturzeitung*
TRev	*Theologische Revue*
TRE	*Theologische Realenzyklopädie*
TZ	*Theologische Zeitschrift*
VT	*Vetus Testamentun*
VTSup	*Vetus Testamentum*, Supplements
WMANT	Wissenschaftliche Monographien zum Alten und Neuen Testament
ZAH	*Zeitschrift für Althebraistik*
ZAW	*Zeitschrift für die alttestamentliche Wissenschaft*
ZDPV	*Zeitschrift des deutschen Palästina-Vereins*

LIST OF CONTRIBUTORS

Diana Edelman
Buffalo Grove, Illinois

Ernst Axel Knauf
University of Heidelberg, Heidelberg

Thomas L. Thompson
Marquette University, Milwaukee

J. Maxwell Miller
Emory University, Atlanta

William G. Dever
University of Arizona, Tucson

Gösta W. Ahlström
The University of Chicago, Chicago

DOING HISTORY IN BIBLICAL STUDIES

Diana Edelman

Introduction

Although we are all familiar with the term 'history', we do not always stop to think about its dimensions and the processes associated with 'doing history' as an investigative discipline. History can designate actual events that transpired in the past, the recoverable traces of actual events that transpired, and the interpretation of past events through the creation of cause-and-effect chains to relate the recoverable traces of those events.[1] The following presentation will focus upon the method associated with the third definition, that involving the discipline devoted to the study of events, changes, and the particularities of our human past through present traces of that past and how historical method is to be applied in biblical studies.

A historical investigation of the events described in the Bible properly belongs to the subdivision of history known as ancient Syro-Palestinian history and within that subdivision, the history of ancient Israel and Judah. Although the term 'biblical history' is often used as a synonym for ancient Near Eastern history or the history of ancient Israel and Judah, strictly speaking, biblical history would be an investigation of the process that led to the formation of the Bible. It would include the drawing of interconnections between particular events over time relating to the writing of individual biblical texts, their joining into larger coherent blocks of material, their organization into books, and the ordering of books to form a comprehensive, canonical piece of sacred literature. By contrast, ancient Syro-Palestinian history is the branch of the study of particular events and changes that took place within the geographical region of ancient Syria–Palestine

---

1. G.R. Elton, *The Practice of History* (New York: Thomas Y. Crowell, 1967), p. 10.

or affected population groups associated with these regions, while the history of ancient Israel and Judah focuses more narrowly on the study of events and changes within the region and among groups associated with the states of Israel and Judah.

Time parameters for the adjective 'ancient' in the term 'ancient Syro-Palestinian history' are determined by consensus rather than by logic or self-evident demands of history itself. The beginning date would be the earliest period from which traces of past human events have been or will be found. The closing date is less easily established; since history is a continuum, the fixing of all subdivisional points within it is arbitrary to some degree and becomes a matter of convention. Generally, events that took place during the time span when Rome controlled most of the ancient Near East are considered to qualify as 'ancient'; the Byzantine era usually falls outside the 'ancient' classification. Any human events dating through the end of the 2nd century CE that took place within the geographical region of ancient Syria–Palestine should therefore qualify as potential topics of historical inquiry within the field of ancient Syro-Palestinian history. All events described within the Bible are within the domain of the ancient Syro-Palestinian or ancient Israelite historian. The ancient Israelite historian is free to pursue additional events that impacted on Israel or Judah but which were not mentioned in the Bible; a myriad of additional events not related to those few preserved in the Bible and not restricted to the states of Israel and Judah alone are equally valid topics of investigation for the ancient Syro-Palestinian historian.

1. *The Historical Process*

Studies conducted within the discipline of history are accomplished through a standard multistep process,[1] with the exact set of methods to be employed being multidisciplinary and determined by the nature of the available evidence. Historical investigations begin when historians choose general topics or problems for study. They then immerse themselves in all the potentially relevant source material, making initial evaluations concerning the genuineness of the available evidence. The immersion step is commonly referred to as familiarization

---

1. So, e.g., Elton, *Practice*, pp. 63-67; P. Conkin and R. Stromberg, *The Heritage and Challenge of History* (New York: Dodd and Mead, 1971), pp. 216-17.

and forms the basis for the next step, conceptual invention. As G.R. Elton has noted,

> historical research does not consist, as beginners in particular often suppose, in the pursuit of some particular evidence which will answer a particular question; it consists of an exhaustive, and exhausting, review of everything that may conceivably be germane to a given investigation.[1]

The crucial step of conceptual invention involves the interpretation of the data. The historian, now intimately familiar with the culture and thought habits of the people in the chronological era and geographical region under investigation, uses instinctive understanding and imagination to create a formal construct such as a schema, a convincing pattern or theme, or a crucial causal hypothesis that will link together pieces of evidence to form a coherent pattern of meaning.

> In the last analysis, whether consciously or no, it is always by borrowing from our daily experiences and by shading them, when necessary, with new tints that we derive the elements which help us to restore the past. For here in the present, is immediately perceptible that vibrance of human life which only a great effort of the imagination can restore to the old text.[2]

Historians are aware that they cannot compose a complete or fully sufficient account of the past events they are studying; they know and accept that the causal links they 'discover' are never all those operative and influential at the time.[3] Nevertheless, they are content to be able to make sense of some portion of the complex of past events they are studying by interconnecting the disjointed remains of those events. The interpretive stage is 'the outlet for historical genius, for the man who can meet an age in diverse, fragmentary surviving artifacts, and quickly see a unifying pattern and likely connections'.[4] 'Meaningful interconnection in the particular, illuminating generalization beyond the individual case—these are the marks that distinguish the inspired and inspiring historian from the hack.'[5]

---

1. Elton, *Practice*, pp. 66-67.
2. M. Bloch, *The Historian's Craft* (trans. P. Putnam; New York: Alfred Knopf, 1953), p. 44.
3. For types of causal judgments, see Conkin and Stromberg, *Heritage*, pp. 187-88, 192, 197, 202-203.
4. Conkin and Stromberg, *Heritage*, p. 217.
5. Elton, *Practice*, p. 98.

The next step in a historical investigation involves the inductive verification of the formal interpretive construct. The historian actively seeks to 'flesh out' the unifying pattern with the appropriate evidence. The selected evidence now must be carefully analyzed to establish its genuineness. Questions and problems raised by the formal construct must be answered and solved convincingly. At times, these questions and answers will force the modification of the unifying pattern, as will the analysis of selected evidence. The interpretive process is one that involves fine-tuning through continued examination and consideration of the evidence. The final step, which is not always undertaken, is the communication of the knowledge acquired in the previous steps to others through writing, that is, historiography.

When attempting to understand the past, all disciplines that deal with investigations of past human events must rely on the same body of evidence, the surviving records or artifacts that have been recovered. Historians, archaeologists, social anthropologists, social psychologists, sociologists, economists, and political scientists must all engage in the identical task of critically analyzing the known body of texts and artifacts to establish their forms and to examine the social and individual psychological factors that determine their quality and credibility. Regardless of one's discipline, one must distinguish between the witness of a participant in the events and testimony of others and weigh each type of report accordingly. One must distinguish between evidence that is deliberately transmitted (annals, chronicles, inscriptions, diaries, memoirs, genealogies, ballads, tales, sagas, certain art works) and that which is unconsciously transmitted (human remains, business and administrative records, language, customs and instructions, certain artifacts). One must distinguish between forgeries and genuine documents, in order to assess the usefulness of each item for the investigation at hand. Judgments as to the neutrality and intentionally biased or deceptive nature of records and remains must be made before any text or artifact can be considered to be acceptable evidence for the events under investigation, regardless of one's particular discipline. The date of texts and artifacts must be established in order to evaluate their appropriateness to the investigation at hand.

2. *History and the Social Sciences*

All disciplines investigating past human events will share the same set of methods for evaluating potential evidence for a given set of events, and those methods will vary, depending upon the nature of the recovered remains. In practice, not every investigator will be able to master the requisite methods for evaluating every type of evidence that will be recovered. Different disciplines train their members to analyse materials that are frequently encountered as forms of primary evidence within their areas of concern, but since the recovered material often takes a range of forms that cuts across the particular concerns of many disciplines, few will have the trained expertise necessary to evaluate all available evidence personally. In the case of human, faunal, and botanical remains, investigators in all disciplines studying the past will need to rely on the expertise of trained specialists who can identify types and date remains through radiocarbon dating, established pottery sequences, and other special processes. In the case of documents, all disciplines will be dependent upon the evaluations of linguists, those trained in paleography, and in some cases, literary critics.

How then does one distinguish a historical investigation of a past event or cluster of events from those conducted in connection with the same set of events within social scientific disciplines such as cultural anthropology, archaeology, or sociology? What are the boundaries of a historical investigation, when there is a shared pool of available evidence and the need to use the same set of multidisciplinary methods to evaluate that evidence among the historical, social scientific and literary disciplines? Simply put, history attempts to understand a given problem from the inside; it is ideographic, that is, it particularizes, while social scientific disciplines generally attempt to explain a problem by linking it to the operation of a law or a more complex, multivariable system; they are nomothetic, that is, designed to establish general laws or models.[1]

> History remains essentially a way of looking at data, and asking and answering the question "Why?" in relation to specific occurrences. It seems generally less concerned to establish and test generalizations about

1. Elton, *Practice*, pp. 18, 26-27.

the properties of social institutions than to trace trains of events over time in terms of chains of cause and effect.[1]

Social scientific investigations, on the other hand, have often been designed to put into the background the particulars of actual events that make them unique and to focus instead on those aspects that allow them to be identified with other entities or events of a similar kind and so provide the basis for abstracting behavioral or physical laws or systems governing behavior or reactions. In practice then, there will be a certain degree of overlap in the pieces of the available pool of evidence that will be selected for inclusion in a historical reconstruction and a social scientific one, but inevitably there will also be differences. A historical reconstruction will usually include many more event-specific details.

Within recent decades there has been a visible shift within the focus of many social scientific investigations away from establishing generalizations in the form of laws that tend to establish a single cause-and-effect chain to explain observable phenomena toward the formulation and description of systemic models that recognize the simultaneous operation of a number of variables and cause-and-effect relationships. This has led in turn to a focus on the study of the particulars of a specific society within a delimited time frame. While the shift in emphasis still often maintains the testing and modifications of systemic models as a primary goal, it also seems to reflect the recognition that the idiosyncrasies of different societies are as important as their commonly shared traits. Studies undertaken within the framework of new archaeology are to·be included within the more recent type of social scientific investigation on one of two premises. The artifactual remains recovered through excavation either are to be used 'to discover laws through the testing of their implications', or 'to describe the inner workings of extinct cultural systems in terms of multiple causality and mutual effect'.[2]

Should a social scientist and/or a political scientist decide to investigate Jehu's coup in Judah, for example, their evaluation of available sources would be be made using the identical set of methods that a

1.   I.M. Lewis, 'Introduction', in *History and Social Anthropology* (ed. I.M. Lewis; ASA Monographs, 7; New York: Tavistock, 1968).

2.   F. Hole and R.F. Heizer, *An Introduction to Prehistoric Archeology* (3rd edn; Chicago: Holt, Rinehart & Winston, 1973), pp. 31-37.

historian of Judah would employ. They might even select the same pieces of evidence to include in their reconstructions, so that the final products might seem to be alternative solutions to the same issue, arrived at by using the same methodology. It is likely, however, that each professional's background field would be able to be discerned from the larger context within which the specific investigation was undertaken, the particular set of related problems that are defined and examined, the nature of the cause-and-effect chains or system created to link together the pieces of evidence, and the relative use of theory or generalized law to inform the reconstruction. Investigators coming from a discipline that regularly uses models and theories that have been abstracted from a number of specific case studies will tend to analyze data with such constructs in mind, whether consciously or not.

By contrast, a person undertaking a historical investigation will select and arrange evidence on the basis of the imagination and instinctive judgment of one who, through immersion in the evidence, lives in a past age 'as a contemporary equipped with immunity, hindsight, and arrogant superiority'[1] and so is able to use personal judgment to discern one or more patterns of interrelations, of cause and effect, among as much of the body of evidence as possible. The historian will not have a set of models and theories designed to explain laws of behavior or nature as part of the tools of the historical trade. While individuals will inevitably draw on their entire range of personal experience to select data and link it into causal patterns and so may unconsciously be swayed by knowledge of social scientific models and theories, there will be no conscious and systematic application of a specific theory or model to the evidence. Instead, there will be a tendency to use analogies drawn from personal knowledge or experience that are both consciously and subconsciously perceived to share similarities with specific situations or details under investigation.

At times, the historian may not be able to arrive at a cause-and-effect chain to interrelate the evidence; 'very often he finds that no strategy whatsoever can wring from the fragments that have survived answers to the questions it purports to deal with'.[2] In this case, the historian will abandon the investigation or shift to another topic that

---

1. Elton, *Practice*, p. 17.
2. J.H. Hexter, *Doing History* (Bloomington, IN: Indiana University Press, 1971), p. 109.

might be more conducive to the body of available data. By contrast, social scientists faced with such a situation might employ an established model or theory from their particular field of inquiry to bridge the evidentiary gaps and provide plausible explanations for missing steps in logical causation. In so doing, they would be appealing to an underlying body of analogous events from disparate time periods and cultures whose particulars have been played down or eliminated from consideration in the interest of the establishment of a generalized scientific law. Such a use of theory or model does not invalidate a proposed bridging effort, but neither does it strengthen its results. The lack of essential data cannot be overcome until the data themselves become available, if ever.

Many people presume that a social-scientific approach to humanity's past is somehow 'better' or 'truer' than a historical one because it can relate events to established models of behavior that can be independently tested and verified. However, such an attitude rests on the false premise that there are empirical 'laws' or models governing the march of history, similar to the 'laws' or models of behavior or physical science that are studied within the sciences. There are no such historical 'laws' to be used to explain or deduce the chain of events in an individual case under study. We no longer need to follow in the footsteps of past generations who were

> mesmerized by the Comtian conception of physical science. This hypnotic *schema*, extending to every province of the intellect, seemed to them to prove that no authentic discipline could exist which did not lead, by its immediate and irrefutable demonstrations, to the formulation of absolute certainties in the form of sovereign and universal laws.[1]

In the light of continuing intellectual development, 'we no longer feel obliged to impose upon every subject of knowledge a uniform intellectual pattern, borrowed from natural science, since, even there, that pattern has ceased to be entirely applicable'.[2]

This is not to deny, however, that historians can and often regularly do employ closed generalizations, which consist of time-conditioned, culturally relative but enduring regularities in human behavior. Although they are not concerned with their verification as a social scientist would be, they are very much concerned with their veracity.

1. Bloch, *Historian's Craft*, p. 14.
2. Bloch, *Historian's Craft*, p. 17.

Many social scientists use such closed generalizations for predictive purposes; when they do, they should 'acknowledge a historical rather than a truly "lawful" backdrop for them'.[1]

Since there are no empirical 'laws' governing the historical process, the historian is content to be able to discover some sort of pattern among a chosen set of events through creative reason. Some may object that irrationality can play a role in the fashioning of events so that the creation of causal chains through rational insight is not always legitimate. In reply, one can simply note (as does G.R. Elton) that

> reason does in measure work in men's lives, and on balance actions and motives are much more commonly explained correctly on assumption that some form of thinking has taken place, rather than that they welled up out of some unconscious which defies analysis.[2]

Even if one accepts reason as a legitimate operational tool in a historical enterprise,

> it is easy for a logician to demonstrate the tenuous chain of arguments that mark almost any complex historical judgment. In this sense, much of history is a stab into partial darkness, a matter of informed but inconclusive conjecture. The available evidence rarely necessitates our judgments but is at least consistent with them. Obviously, in such areas of interpretation, there is no one demonstrably correct 'explanation', but very often competing, equally unfalsifiable, theories.[3]

Historians are content to accept the tentativeness of their insights and the need to modify, adjust, or abandon their interpretations of the evidence in light of new evidence or a better interpretive framework.

3. The Task of the Ancient Israelite Historian

The ancient Syro-Palestinian or ancient Israelite historian who chooses to study an event described in the Bible will need to utilize the following range of methods associated with different disciplines, intersecting partially or sometimes totally with the other disciplines' concerns. After choosing a general topic for investigation, he or she must set about establishing a pool of potentially relevant evidence. The easiest place to begin is with the pertinent biblical account(s) and then

1. Conkin and Stromberg, *Heritage*, p. 165.
2. Elton, *Practice*, p. 98.
3. Conkin and Stromberg, *Heritage*, p. 219.

to move on to any extant extrabiblical texts deemed potentially relevant to the chosen topic. The process of evaluation will be identical for all literary evidence.

After reading the texts, the historian must establish what parts of the narrative are reliable evidence and what parts are fictional embellishment and ideological rhetoric. To do this, one must employ a number of methods developed by the discipline of literary studies: text criticism, to establish the definitive text to be used; literary criticism, to establish the structural and literary devices used to create the final form of the narrative, to spot any internal inconsistencies that might indicate later reworking, to understand authorial intentions, and to deduce a possible date of composition; form criticism, to understand the genres of literature found within the narrative as possible clues to the author's life-setting or the life-setting of possible sources used to create the narrative; and finally, source criticism, to move behind the final form of the text and discover what possible types of sources could have been available to the author, what kinds were likely to have existed, their date, which ones were likely to have been used and why.

Historians must either personally master all of the skills necessary to perform all of the above methods of evaluation or must rely upon the expertise of literary scholars for whatever methods they are unable to employ with confidence themselves. While a text-critical, literary-critical, form-critical, or source-critical analysis can stand on its own within the field of literary studies, for the historian, each is a necessary, initial, and incomplete step in the sorting of fact from fiction in the quest to judge the genuineness of details in the selected group of texts. Historians will have completed a literary analysis of all of the potentially pertinent texts, but their communication of findings, their historiographic reconstructions of the chosen events, will not necessarily describe in detail the stages of literary analysis. Instead, they will build upon the results of the literary evaluation by employing what has been judged to be genuine evidence, possibly placing limited analytical arguments in footnotes.

In addition to literary evidence, ancient Syro-Palestinian and ancient Israelite historians usually have at their disposal potentially relevant artifactual evidence that has been gathered through surface surveys and site excavations. After deciding on the appropriate chronological and geographical frames, historians must sift through the available remains. If not themselves experts in pottery forms or chronology, or in faunal and floral identification, they will have to rely upon the judgments of experts within these areas and their published findings in initial and final archaeological excavation and survey reports. Nevertheless, it is crucial for every historian to read such reports critically to be sure that all judgments of date and identification have been made on the basis of appropriate criteria—context, and comparative stratigraphy and morphology. Historians also need to be familiar enough with the goals and limitations of archaeological methods that they can judge the relative strengths and weaknesses of artifactual evidence and assign appropriate weight to the evidence for their own investigations.

At times, an archaeologist will use the Bible or other textual materials inappropriately to date or identify remains, confusing the initial task of reporting finds and identifying levels of occupation with the final task of undertaking a reconstruction of the history of the excavated site—whether in terms of describing its workings as a system or of testing the implication of laws, premises, or systems through recovered data. It is only here, in the final step involving the reconstruction of the past—however that reconstruction is framed—that a synthesis of artifacts and occupational remains with relevant textual evidence, itself fully criticized by the investigator or literary experts, is to take place. The archaeologist must now employ historical methodology, or defer to a historian able to do so, immersing himself or herself fully in the evidence, linking it through creative reason, and fleshing out the resulting pattern with appropriate details. It is particularly crucial that the archaeologist should not fall into the trap of importing a social scientific model or system to explain the data and create cause-and-effect relationships when his goal is historical reconstruction. This is an easy and safe way out for one not trained in the use of creative reason, but the results will be disastrous, eliminating the particulars that make history history.

Having evaluated the potential pool of evidence, the historian is now ready for familiarization, conceptual invention, and inductive verification. Some scholars may prefer to delay their reading of other secondary discussions and proposed solutions to the problem until after they have worked through the primary evidence and arrived at their own tentative solutions. Others may prefer to have read the secondary discussions prior to launching their personal investigation. At times, dissatisfaction with existing explanations will prompt historians to undertake a new investigation of a topic. Secondary discussions by other historians, literary scholars and social scientists can often serve as invaluable aids to focus one's attention or improve one's grasp of the full breadth of the problem. Subtle relationships that the historian might not have personally considered in the familiarization process may have been noted by others and can now be incorporated into his or her own interpretive framework or in the inductive verification process, with due credit given in footnote citations. At other times, observations made by others will challenge the historian's own tentative conclusions and force the modification of the initial interpretive scheme.

At whatever point historians decide to evaluate secondary reconstructions by colleagues in their own and related fields, it is essential that such an enterprise be undertaken before they reach their final interpretation of the evidence and any historiographic presentation of their findings. The secondary reconstructions themselves form a secondary pool of 'evidence' for the crucial interpretive stage of the historical process, the stage that is based on creative invention. While there is always the danger that a historian will unconsciously impose a pattern on the artifactual and textual evidence that has been primarily influenced by other interpretations of the evidence rather than by the evidence itself, the results will speak for themselves. If the proposed interpretation is able to integrate as much of the evidence as possible into a coherent and plausible cause-and-effect pattern, then the proposed solution will be deemed successful, whatever the source of its inspiration. In theory, the evidence should be the primary source for inspiration and the interpretive insights of others a secondary source for further refinement of insights initially formulated from an encounter with the evidence.

4. Conclusion

What then are the boundaries of historical method within biblical studies? Any topic dealing with events, changes and the particulars of the human past that are mentioned within the Bible, one source providing potential traces of the past within the subdiscipline of ancient Syro-Palestinian history, is fair game. The topic will usually focus on an attempt to answer the question 'why' in relationship to a constellation of circumstances involving who, what, when and where, all of which must also be established. A historical-critical investigation will need to include the main steps of familiarization, conceptual invention, and inductive verification of the formal interpretive construct through the use of the evidence, not through an appeal to generalized 'laws'. The specific set of methods used as evaluative tools will be determined by the nature of the potentially relevant evidence available and so will vary from topic to topic. Always included will be text criticism, literary criticism, form criticism, and source criticism, because the Bible will be one, if not the main, source of literary evidence. Should artifactual evidence be available, which it generally is, then methods for identifying and processing artifacts within the fields of archaeology and related scientific disciplines such as paleobotany and zooarchaeology will also be necessary.

'In the last analysis, it is human consciousness which is the subject matter of history. The interrelations, confusions and infections of human consciousness are, for the historian, reality itself.'[1]

---

1.   Bloch, *Historian's Craft*, p. 151.

Ernst Axel Knauf

1. *Prolegomena*

There are two compartments in heaven: a big one, advertised as 'heaven', where you are going to meet just about everybody, and a small one with a huge billboard reading 'Introduction to the Theory of Heaven'. There you'll find the Germans.

It is the purpose of this contribution to evaluate the interpretive potential of historical criticism for biblical studies. It may be stated in advance that the more Israel's ancient history differs from the biblical narrative, the higher the explanatory potential of history in elucidating that narrative's origin and purpose would be. We have to know history before we can interpret ancient texts (or artifacts) historically. But how can we know history?

History and the Past

We cannot know the past, for the past is gone. Whatever is past is irretrievably lost, abducted by the irreversible flow of human time. All that we can examine are the present remnants of the past: memories and relics, stories and material remains. People's present memory of their individual or collective past is a *present* memory, and is not identical with what has been memorized, which is no longer present. Furthermore, history as organized collective memory is, like any other kind of human memory, always more influenced by present interests and self-appreciation than by the events of yesteryears; I will shortly elaborate on this aspect. Relics of the things that happened to have existed form a small, poor, and usually nonrepresentative sample of all things past. Furthermore, relics are as mute as ancient texts if not perceived within an interpretive framework that bestows upon them meaning and significance. Meaning and significance do not exist outside the human mind (with the possible exception of the minds of gods and angels which, however, are entities beyond the scope of a scholarly discussion). Every history is the creation of a human mind.

Epistemological discussions of history cannot move beyond the question of how to create history responsibly, which immediately leads to the question: responsible to which set of standards? I intend to describe how history is and how it can be created; I do not intend to prescribe how it should be created. The inventiveness and imagination of historians will always elude the categories of the theoretician, and happily so. However, I have to maintain that every creation of history has moral and political implications besides purely intellectual ones. That history cannot exist in any other form than a variety of competing histories, regardless of whether we are dealing with ancient Israel's history or that of modern Europe, should already be evident (for those who doubt this basic fact, there is the book market to convince them).[1]

Objective History
The remnants of the past, texts and artifacts alike, are not identical with the past. History is not identical with the sources. History is not even in the sources, which was a sound insight of the 19th century.[2] If history does not exist except in our minds, the creation of history raises a moral issue, for we alone are responsible for the kind of history that we construct.

A widespread attitude encountered in continental biblical history

---

1. According to my observations (based on a broad, if by no means representative sample), the vast majority of German students is still learning 'history of Israel' from outdated textbooks because these happen to be short, cheap, and intellectually nondemanding. That few of them fail their exams might testify to the low significance of history within their examiners' demands, or to a widespread misconception of intellectual pluralism: that there always is a variety of potentially right theories available does not mean that every theory is potentially right. Important as the aspect of the distribution of historical knowledge is, the remnant of this essay will concentrate on the production of historical knowledge.

2. Cf. J.G. Droysen's letter to F. Perthes of the 8th February 1837 as quoted by K. Christ, *Von Gibbon zu Rostovtzeff. Leben und Werk führender Althistoriker der Neuzeit* (Darmstadt: Wissenschaftliche Buchgesellschaft, 1979), p. 65: 'Das wahre Faktum steht nicht in den Quellen. . . Man braucht einen höheren Gesichtspunkt als das Kritisieren der Quellen'.

writing is the claim that one's reconstruction does not contradict, or even agrees with, the Bible.[1] As will be discussed, this attitude usually refuses to consider its own theoretical presuppositions. It tries to delegate responsibility from the historians to one of their sources. As this particular source, the Bible, is held to be of utmost authority by western religions (a fact known and respected by any historian, but nevertheless irrelevant for historical interpretation), this attitude may easily appear to be an attempt to furnish the individual historian's reconstruction with a higher authority than any scholarly construct can claim.

The claim also seems to be an easy and rather irresponsible way out of the problem that history, including biblical history, only exists as conflicting histories proposed by various historians or historical schools. On the other hand, historians of the 20th century CE who claim to agree with historians of the 5th century BCE (or, to be precise, with what they consciously or subconsciously reconstruct as the ancient historians' view) may sound rather suspicious to those historians who maintain that there has been some progress in the field of historiographical theory-building within the past 2500 years, not to speak of the accumulating primary evidence provided by archaeology and epigraphy that was not available to our ancient colleagues. Admittedly, the vicious hermeneutical circle raises its none too handsome head at such a point: if history is based on the interpretation of sources, and historical interpretation is based on the theoretical approach of the historians that in turn is based on their previous knowledge of history, there seems to be no way rationally to choose between conflicting histories. So everything goes? No. For 'objective history' is possible—or rather, it is possible to construct history in accordance with the principles of objective knowledge.

There is no history that is not a human creation—a position which can be found *in nuce* in St Augustine's reflections about the nature of time.[2] Although every history is a theoretical construct, not every

---

1. For a critical view of that attitude, exemplified by the work of one of its major adherents, see B.J. Diebner, ' "Steht nicht im Gegensatz zur biblischen Tradition." Review of S. Herrmann, "Geschichte Israels", *TRE* XII (1984), pp. 698-740', in *DBAT* 19 (1984), pp. 147-53; cf. also *idem*, '"Es lässt sich nicht beweisen, Tatsache aber ist. . ." Sprachfigur statt Methode in der kritischen Erforschung des AT', *DBAT* 18 (1984), pp. 138-46.

2. Cf. Augustine, *Confessiones* 11.14.17-20.26; 27.35–30.40.

theory is a critical, that is, self-improving theory. Knowledge is the human response to the experience of that real world beyond our senses and beyond our intellect that we do not and cannot know. But knowledge is not necessarily objective. Objective knowledge is the transient and preliminary, but momentarily valid product of the self-critical dialogue between hypothesis and test, theory and experience. In our constant encounter with the unknown we can never know the 'truth' (which would actually presuppose that we were God; nevertheless, possession of the 'final truth' is frequently claimed. . .). We can only eliminate the 'wrong' from our theories by perpetual testing—which presupposes that we do not admit statements that cannot be tested. Every scientific statement is potentially wrong.[1]

We do not find knowledge, we make it. The concept of knowledge as a product of the human mind contrasts with the Platonic-Aristotelian concept of knowledge as an adaptation of the mind to some pre-existent truth. The 'bucket' or 'mirror theory' of the intellect, as it was authoritatively summarized by St Thomas,[2] gave rise to the beginnings of western rationality and the basic concept of scientific research, as it challenged William Occam to apply his razor: *entia non sunt multiplicanda praeter necessitatem*. However, residues of Thomasian 'realism' still linger in the back of many researchers' minds. These residues surface whenever scholars claim to proceed from facts to theories[3] without regard to their default theories that produced their 'facts' in the first place; they also surface whenever hypotheses are discredited for their simply being such—as if there were any knowledge that is not hypothetical in nature;[4] and they

1. Cf. K.R. Popper, *Objective Knowledge* (Oxford: Clarendon Press, 1972); idem, *The Logic of Scientific Discovery* (8th rev. edn; London: Hutchinson, 1975). I hope that the brevity of my paraphrase does not produce too great a distortion of Sir Karl's basic thoughts.
2. Cf. St Thomas Aquinas, *Summa contra gentiles*, 2.59-62, 67, 73-78.
3. For the 19th-century background to this attitude, still firmly rooted in Aristotelian epistemology and still quite virulent today, see L.L. Stevenson, *Scholarly Means to Evangelical Ends. The New Haven Scholars and the Transformation of Higher Learning in America, 1830–1890* (Baltimore and London: Johns Hopkins University Press, 1986), pp. 12-39.
4. Primary examples for this attitude are provided every four months by the 'Zeitschriften-und Bücherschau' of *ZAW*.

definitely surface whenever somebody's belief in 'lasting' (ever-lasting?) results of scholarly work is expressed.

The acknowledgment that facts are theoretical constructs would highly facilitate the discussion between conflicting theories and par-tially unburden scholars from ignoring their opponents—or from charging them with stupidity, the deficit of knowing enough facts, or illwill, the refusal to acknowledge facts for what they are (although scholars are no more immune to those intellectual deficits than is the general public). For the archaeologist who has a theory about the significance of undecorated pottery, or the floral and faunal contents of soil samples, sherds and soil samples are facts; for the art historian, they are just rubbish. Especially in the case of ceramic samples, it is obvious that their historical significance rests with the theory that attributes chronological and cultural values to them.[1] It is less obvious but equally valid that the historical significance of texts is just as dependent on the interpreters' presuppositions.[2]

Following the epistemology of K.R. Popper, history can be con-structed as objectively and as scientifically as any other area of human knowledge. This does not mean that every history is, or can, or has to be objective. Everyday language still speaks of a rising sun and not of a revolving earth. Traditional history—the history in the back of everyone's mind—is not objective, although in enlightened cultures it increasingly intends or at least claims to be; nor is any piece of ancient history objective in the sense that these historians tried to formulate statements that could be disproved by their sources. The difference between an objective, scientific history and a nonscientific history is

---

1.   Although Edomite sherds have not changed their appearance or consistency between 1934 and 1989, our understanding of what an 'Edomite' sherd is and what its occurrence at a site means has changed considerably, and without doubt is going to change further; cf. J.R. Bartlett, *Edom and the Edomites* (JSOTSup, 77; Sheffield: JSOT Press, 1989), pp. 70-74, 132-135.

2.   This is obvious in the case of the Hebrew Bible, and it has long been observed how assumptions about the date and nature of a text determine its historical evaluation. Contrast, e.g., the different approaches to the patriarchal narratives, or, more concretely, the problem of the location of Heshbon (see below) or the temporal and spatial definition of the tribe of Simeon (S. Mittmann, 'Ri. 1,16f und das Siedlungsgebiet der kenitischen Sippe Hobab', *ZDPV* 93 [1977], pp. 217-18). For the text as an open parameter in historical evaluations, see also E.A. Knauf, 'Pireathon—Fer'atā', *BN* 51 (1990), pp. 19-24.

not that the scientific historian is without presuppositions. The difference is that in scientific history the theory is as disputable as the facts are; the presuppositions are conceived to be debatable to the same extent that any statement derived from them is. Only ideologists are always right; scholars know that everything they say is potentially wrong (if it were not, they would have committed the unforgivable sin against the holy ghost of scholarship of making statements that cannot be tested). Scholars are aware that there is no security to be gained in real-world studies and that 50 per cent of this generation's intellectual achievements will be disregarded by the next generation in much the same way as this generation has dealt—and is dealing—with the giants on whose shoulders we stand.

Closed intellectual systems, like ideologies, prefer to disregard large amounts of primary evidence rather than change or abandon the system. Does Galileo's telescope reveal moons around Jupiter? Since it is an established truth that by his metaphysical nature Jupiter cannot have moons, there is no point in looking through a telescope! Does anthropology not agree with Alt, nor Albright? Then anthropology must surely be wrong, or at least not be applicable to the world of 3000 years ago! Sooner or later, closed systems collapse, usually at the moment when they no longer muster the power to accommodate the world to their concepts.[1] The ability to adapt to a changing world

---

1.   A primary example of the fatal consequences of a closed intellectual system is provided by the demise of imperial China: R. Hoffmann, *Der Untergang des konfuzianischen China* (Wiesbaden: Otto Harrassowitz, 1980). A similar mechanism of intellectual nonadaptability may explain the quick breakdown of the Assyrian empire between 628 and 609 BCE (some evidence pointing towards such a mechanism at play is collected, if not totally analyzed, by H. Spieckermann, *Juda unter Assur in der Sargonidenzeit* [Göttingen: Vandenhoeck & Ruprecht, 1982]). In the historical narrative that reflects the culture's appreciation of itself the Chinese emperor and the Assyrian king were always victorious; as soon as it became evident to too many people that sometimes they were not, there was no emperor and no king any more. One may also compare the different attitudes of Britain and Russia in and after the Crimean war, when facing an identical problem, i.e., the inadequacy of a Napoleonic military organization one generation after Napoleon's death: 'The chorus which sounded from the British camp was a spur for action, both by the army and the government in London. Its eventual consequence was the improvement of organization and conditions by a system which was capable of accepting criticism and acting upon it. In Russia the baleful news of setbacks and errors produced only despair. . .' (L. James, *Crimea 1854–56. The War with Russia from Contemporary*

favors objective knowledge as opposed to beliefs; security is the price to be paid, which explains why, in a highly civilized and very complex world such as the present one, fundamentalism is such a temptation.

Objectivity in history does not mean that historians who try to constitute objective history do not pursue philosophical, moral, religious or political purposes in their work.[1] On the contrary: the acquisition and spread of objective knowledge actually is a moral and political issue. It is a moral issue insofar as humanity, individually as well as collectively, is to be held responsible for their deeds (yes, it is the historian's task to analyze and theoretically, to explain everything, including the holocaust; but to understand in no way means to excuse!). Moral responsibility includes the responsibility to know what can be known and then to act.[2] The spread of objective knowledge forms a political issue insofar as rationality, its guarding principle, is the only universal mode of communication.[3] Opting for this mode implies opting for the maximal participation of the maximal

Photographs [New York: Van Nostrand, 1981], p. 29).

1.   For misconceived objectivity and its fallibility, cf. P. Novick, *That Noble Dream. The 'Objectivity Question' and the American Historical Profession* (Cambridge: Cambridge University Press, 1988). Ranke's fundamental question, 'How did it really happen?', is nonsensical insofar as we cannot know the reality of the past. The question can be rephrased as 'What can we reasonably assume to have happened?' and then can serve as a primary catalyst for distinguishing processes and events from their reflection in narrative traditions. 'Objectivity in history' cannot mean more than the attempt of historians to formulate conjectures that the sources can refute and to mark clearly statements that do not conform to the requirements of objectivity (but nevertheless are an important part of their thoughts and help to elucidate their purposes).

2.   'The one thing in war—as in life—is to guess what is on the other side of the hill', the first Duke of Wellington supposedly said.

3.   For rationality as the only universal catholicism, see I. Kant, *Der Streit der Fakultäten in drey Abschnitten* (Königsberg: F. Nicolovius, 1798), pp. 73-74: W. Weischedel (ed.), *Immanuel Kant Werkausgabe*, XI (Frankfurt: Surhkamp, 1968), pp. 316-17. Needless to say, the book was indexed. The political implications of Popper's epistemology are as obvious: cf. K.R. Popper, *The Open Society and its Enemies* (2 vols.; Princeton, NJ: Princeton University Press, 1971). A German predecessor of Braudel, Karl Lamprecht (1856–1915) was ousted from that country's historiographical tradition under the charge of 'decadent western democratic concepts' (cf. H. Schleier (ed.), *Karl Lamprecht—Alternative zu Ranke. Schriften zur Geschichtstheorie* [Leipzig: Reclam, 1988], p. 19). Cf. also S. Rosen, *Hermeneutics as Politics* (New York and Oxford: Oxford University Press, 1987).

number of people in the process of knowledge (and decision-making). One cannot have intellectual freedom, the primary requisite of scholarly efficiency, without civil liberties. One cannot 'learn' scholarship without learning to question every theoretical statement, be it received or self-produced, time and again. Whoever learned to think critically will not and cannot leave this mode of thinking at the hatrack next to the office door, but necessarily carries the dynamite of intellectual evolution to the broader public. Societies that tried otherwise had to learn this basic fact the hard way[1]—and I dare to predict that contemporary closed societies will have to learn it the same way.

Whosoever wishes may call the concept of objective knowledge and its underlying principles of rational discourse and individual freedom (i.e. responsibility) elements of another ideology, conceived by European culture in order to dominate the world to the detriment of non-European cultures. I can half agree with the first part of such a statement: yes, objective knowledge, rational discourse, and inalienable human rights are part and parcel of the set of values that makes me study history (among other things). To be a scholar cannot imply that I have no values, or no cultural pride, or that I am not allowed to talk about them. With the second half I can only disagree (although a majority of this world's population may be inclined to subscribe to such a view). Thinking within a frame of reference that invites and actually facilitates participation irrespective of the participants' race, first language, religion and political convictions renders the question of its inventors' race, first language, religion and political conviction quite irrelevant. The extent to which this system actually rules the world (I wish it would!) is proof of its efficiency rather than the malevolence of its conceivers. Even for those who cherish the ideal of one peaceful world, there remains something for which to fight, as the quest for knowledge—like the quest for the past—is never final.

Like historians, people have choices in setting the parameters for their default hypotheses. In setting their parameters, they inevitably take sides. I side with the unlimited freedom of the individual, this most fragile and most basic hypostasis of what we are, to put every-

---

1.   German intellectual life never recovered—and is unlikely ever to recover—from 1933 and the enforced exodus of its better half. For self-destroying strategies pursued to total success by a different closed intellectual system, one may refer to the present state of eastern Europe.

thing to the test of rationality. I oppose the physical and intellectual restrictions that always threaten our freedom apart from those restrictions deriving from the equal rights of every other person. I opt for rationality as the only mode of communication that respects the equality of all communicators, as opposed to irrational, that is, sectarian demands. If these options are something to fight about, I am perfectly willing to do so.

As a result, I cannot agree with the (growing?) number of historians and anthropologists whose goal is to interpret foreign cultures—and every past culture is a very foreign culture—'in their own terms'. Since no other culture has developed the analytical tools to achieve objective knowledge as described above, this claim is void at best and possibly no more than a thin disguise for unclaimed, undiscussed, and uncriticized personal inferences by the researcher.[1] To be sure, other cultures, past and present, were and are different. Rational analysis will demonstrate as precisely as possible how different they are. To think in their terms is both undesirable and, in the case of past cultures, impossible (given the incomplete and usually nonrepresentative record). A manuscript of 250 pages in Sumerian is by no means a doctoral dissertation in Sumeriology.

Excursus: Prediction in History
There is no structural difference between the disciplines of science and the humanities. Both proceed by conjecture and refutation, and both result in theories that interpret reality (and are equally far from being identical with that reality). Present cosmological theories are as much a human understanding of the universe (different from the universe itself) as historical endeavors are an attempt to understand the past according to material or immaterial remnants of the past (which are different from the past itself). If there is any difference between the sciences and the humanities, it lies in the easier accessibility of tests in the sciences. For historians, digging through unexplored archives or excavation reports is the equivalent of the experiments of their scientist colleagues. Admittedly, the data base in humanities is more limited and statements are accordingly less thoroughly tested.

---

1.   M. Harris (*Cultural Materialism. The Struggle for a Science of Culture* [New York: Random House, 1980], pp. 315-41) aptly characterizes nonrational approaches as what they are: obscurantism.

But the data base of scientists is not unlimited either.

There remains the objection that there exist no 'laws' in history. Attempts to produce them have proven to be futile.[1] However, this claim seems to be based on a naïve misconception of 'laws' in physics. Basically, laws are generalizations that lead to definite expectations, which in turn can be formulated as predictions.

On the analytical level of generalizations and predictions, history is no different than the sciences. History works with generalizations, sometimes disguised as analogies. Generalizations about the process of political evolution, or the spread of a new religion (or, for that matter, a new brand of toothpaste) are possible.[2] So are predictions.

1.   Cf. K.R. Popper, *The Poverty of Historicism* (New York: Harper & Row, 1964). The term 'historicism' (in the German translation, unfortunately, rendered as as 'Historizismus') was coined by Popper to denote deterministic theories extending the past into the future. This attitude is contrary to the approach of historism (in German, 'Historizismus' in its established meaning), which in its milder form stresses that people of the past thought in terms and acted on principles quite different from our own, which is only too true. In a more dogmatic way, historism likes to stress the nondurability of all cultures and their cultural products, including those that coincidentally still exist. This is a thought which, regarded from the point of view of our own mortality, is quite likely to be true (although the final test would presuppose a vantage point from outside of time, and therefore is impossible)—and is very healthy anyway. In its radical form, historism denies that there are any anthropological universals. Whether this assumption is true or not can never be decided (because complete knowledge of all human cultures past and present cannot be achieved). Even if there may be none, participation in the search for anthropological universals is an important aspect of the historians' task. History that does not try to arrive at generalizations (as, e.g., the mechanics of state formation) would not be, in my opinion, history at all, but antiquarianism, which boils down to running an intellectual curiosity shop with no more relevance to society at large than providing entertainment for the idle, the jaded and the doomed.

2.   The relevance of anthropological generalizations about political evolution, such as those offered by M.H. Fried (*The Evolution of Political Society. An Essay in Political Anthropology* [New York: Random House, 1967]) and E.R. Service (*Origins of the State and Civilization. The Process of Cultural Evolution* [New York: Norton, 1975]), has been amply demonstrated by recent work on the early history of Israel (e.g. F.S. Frick, *The Formation of the State in Ancient Israel. A Survey of Models and Theories* [SWBAS, 4; Sheffield: Almond Press, 1985] and R.B. Coote and K.W. Whitelam, *The Emergence of Early Israel in Historical Perspective* [SWBAS, 5; Sheffield: Almond Press, 1987]), although continuing research will probably have to elaborate on the differences between primary state formation

Of course it is impossible to predict the future of any society from its past, although predictions of what is going to happen if present modes of behavior continue are possible. Predictions like these are, however, usually made with the purpose of making people change their behavior. For professional historiography, it is not possible to make predictions outside historical space, that is, the past, but it is perfectly possible to make predictions, that is, to formulate expectations, within historical space. As an example, I will take the liberty to formulate some predictions based on my present understanding of Arabian cultural history before Islam.[1] Proto-Arabic inscriptions dating from the 12th through 7th centuries BCE will be found in northwest and west Arabia and will provide the 'missing link' between the proto-Canaanite and south Semitic scripts; none of the architectural or inscriptional appurtenances of state societies will be found in south Arabia prior to the 8th century BCE; more ancient north Arabian inscriptions written by Nabataeans will be found (for the time being, only one is known); inscriptions that characterize the same individual as both a Qedarite and a Nabataean will be found. To place a bet in the

(as studied by Fried and Service) and secondary state formation (cf. B.J. Price, 'Secondary State Formation: An Explanatory Model', in *The Origins of State: The Anthropology of Political Evolution* [ed. R. Cohen and E.R. Service; Philadelphia: Institute for the Study of Human Issues, 1978], pp. 161-86). A fine example of extrapolation in history (based on disputable data, but using a convincing theoretical approach) has been provided by R.W. Bulliet, *Conversion to Islam in the Medieval Period. An Essay in Quantitative History* (Cambridge, MA; Harvard University Press, 1979). Extrapolation is by no means unscientific; quite the contrary: no physicist ever saw or will ever be able to see a quark. For the reasons given above, I cannot agree with N.P. Lemche, *Early Israel. Anthropological and Historical Studies on the Israelite Society before the Monarchy* (VTSup, 37; Leiden: Brill, 1985), pp. 216-19. I see no nonobscurantist alternative to a systemic and an evolutionary approach to any aspect of past or present humanity.

1.   The following predictions are based on E.A. Knauf, *Midian. Untersuchungen zur Geschichte Palästinas und Nordarabiens am Ende des 2. Jahrtausends v. Chr.* (ADPV; Wiesbaden: Otto Harrassowitz, 1988); idem, 'The West Arabian Place Name Province: Its Origin and Significance', *Proceedings of the Seminar for Arabian Studies* 18 (1988), pp. 39-49; idem, *Ismael. Untersuchungen zur Geschichte Palästinas und Nordarabiens im 1. Jahrtausend v. Chr.* (2nd enlarged edn; ADPV; Wiesbaden: Otto Harrassowitz, 1989); idem, 'The Migration of the Script, and the Formation of the State in South Arabia', *Proceedings of the Seminar for Arabian Studies* 19 (1989), pp. 79-91.

realm of biblical history: if Saul or David ever appear in a dated, contemporary inscription their reign will turn out to be closer to 950 BCE rather than 1000 BCE.[1]

The Levels of History

In constituting history, it is the historian—or the uncritical mind—who calls the shots. History is not in the sources; the sources are the universe in which the historian's hypotheses are tested. For the uncritical mind's perception of history, sources are not relevant at all because this mind does not want to test its perceptions. One of the attitudes most detrimental to the discussion of the issues that really are at stake is the widespread habit of the awareness of one's own theoretical *a prioris*, or the disguising of theoretical assumptions as statements about facts. Most of my German colleagues still believe in a 'nomadic origin' of Israel and claim that this is what the Bible says. People who do not share the 'nomadic origin theory' don't find it in the Bible either.[2]

Because it is the historians' questions and, therefore, their interests that constitute history, two people may say 'history' and still not mean the same thing. The difficulty that arises from the fact that 'history' always is 'somebody's history of something' may well be illustrated by

1. For the chronology of the first Israelite kings, see my forthcoming article 'King Solomon's Copper Supply', in *Phoenicia and the Bible* (ed. E. Lipiński; Leuven: Peeters).

2. The 'nomadic origin theory' that is tenaciously defended by W. Thiel (*Die soziale Entwicklung Israels in vorstaatlicher Zeit* [2nd edn; Neukirchen–Vluyn: Neukirchener Verlag, 1985], pp. 31-51; and 'Vom revolutionären zum evolutionären Israel?', *TLZ* 113 [1988], pp. 401-10) or A. Malamat (*Mari and the Early Israelite Experience* [The Schweich Lectures, 1984; Oxford: Oxford University Press, 1989]) is anchored in an interpretation of the patriarchal narratives as depicting nomads in the process of settlement. This interpretation is by no means convincing; with the exception of the earliest components in Gen. 18, it is hardly tenable at all; cf. my forthcoming article 'Bedouin and Bedouin States' in the *Anchor Bible Dictionary*. In Gen. 12 and 13, Abraham is far from being a poor 'semi-nomad'; on the contrary, he is depicted as a rich herding-capitalist following the model provided by Nabal of Meon (1 Sam. 25) and Job (Job 1). One may also recall Albright's interpretation of the patriarchs as 'donkey caravaneers'. Although his hypothesis does not pass the test of the available evidence (cf. M. Weippert, 'Abraham der Hebräer? Bemerkungen zu W.F. Albrights Deutung der Vater Israels', *Bib* 52 [1971], pp. 407-31), it cannot be refuted on the basis of the biblical texts.

the history of the use of archaeology in biblical studies.

As long as the Platonic–Aristotelian concept of historical knowledge prevailed, which basically meant 'there is history, and only one history, somewhere, and all we have to do is to find a way to get it into our mind', the basic view was that everything of importance in ancient Israel's history has been narrated in the Bible (and what is not recorded is nowhere and cannot be known). The only task of the historian then was to renarrate that story—minus minor corrections, omissions, and additions due to the growing corpus of external evidence and due to changing views about, for instance, the ability of water to form a solid wall to the right and to the left in order that somebody might cross a waterway without a vessel or the ability to swim. The potential of biblical archaeology to add more details (and color) to a history that was essentially known and had only to be certified and amplified was initially, euphorically cherished.[1]

Now that the first hundred years of the biblical–archaeological endeavor are concluded, not much euphoria is left. The 'history-cum-additions' model of the increase in historical knowledge did not work. Far from silencing the critics' questions and answering the questions that even the uncritical have regarding the historical plausibility of the biblical narrative, archaeology has increased our difficulties with the historicity of biblical historiography considerably. Archaeology (and linguistics, in this case) is unable to trace the culture of those areas that are understood to have been populated by Israelites around 1000 BCE to any other area but Palestine. Concomitantly, no cities existed

1.   In the short but rich history of 'biblical archaeology', the enthusiastic claim of bible-plus-spade scholarship of being able to excavate 'biblical history' has given way to biblical scholars who apply empirical data concerning the linguistic, cultural, economical and political setting of biblical texts to their elucidation (e.g. P.J. King, *Amos, Hosea, Micah—An Archaeological Commentary* [Philadelphia: Westminster Press, 1988])—or who excavate Palestinian cultural history with due regard for areas and periods that are well outside the scope of the Bible (cf. p. 45 n. 1). Both research programs make sense, and although it is by no means impossible that the same person is engaged in both, the number of scholars who will be able to do so will undoubtedly further decline as the material and the methods to be mastered in any field are continuously increasing. The ideological and political environment of early 'biblical archaeology' and its gradual shift in focus from the Bible to the land is well described by N.A. Silberman, *Digging for God and Country. Exploration, Archaeology, and the Secret Struggle for the Holy Land, 1799–1917* (New York: A.A. Knopf, 1982).

on the sites of earlier and later Heshbon, Jericho and Ai when the Israelites were believed to have passed by and conquered them.[1] Archaeologically speaking, there are no indications of statehood being achieved before the 9th century BCE in Israel and the 8th century BCE in Judah[2]—so much for King Solomon in all his splendor. Archaeology is very rarely in a position to answer the question of who, if anybody, destroyed a city. In some cases, however, archaeology can state that there was no destruction of the kind suggested by a literary source.[3] Almost never is it possible to identify the nationality of a cooking pot.[4] Literature and archaeology just do not meet.

1. Among those historians who are acquainted with the primary data, the fact of Israel's emergence from Canaan and within Palestine is no longer disputed; see Lemche, *Early Israel*; G.W. Ahlström, *Who Were the Israelites?* (Winona Lake, IN: Eisenbrauns, 1986); Coote and Whitelam, *The Emergence of Early Israel*; V. Fritz, 'Conquest or Settlement? The Early Iron Age in Palestine', *BA* 50 (1987), pp. 84-100; R.G. Boling, *The Early Biblical Community in Transjordan* (SWBAS, 6; Sheffield: Almond Press, 1988); I. Finkelstein, *The Archaeology of the Israelite Settlement* (Jerusalem: Israel Exploration Society, 1988); E.A. Knauf, 'Zur Herkunft und Sozialgeschichte Israels. "Das Böckchen in der Milch seiner Mutter"', *Bib* 69 (1988), pp. 153-69; J.A. Callaway, 'The Settlement in Canaan', in *Ancient Israel. A Short History from Abraham to the Roman Destruction of the Temple* (ed. H. Shanks; Washington, DC: Biblical Archaeology Society, 1988), pp. 53-84. Disputable is the 'how' (one cannot fail to observe that Finkelstein's version of the 'nomadic origin theory', although archaeologically and anthropologically sound, is based on a circular argument when he first defines 'Israel' as that nomadic segment of Greater Canaan's society that settled down and then concludes that Israel emerged from the settlement of 'nomads'). More books on the subject are eagerly anticipated.

2. Cf. D.W. Jamieson-Drake, *Scribes and Schools in Monarchic Judah: A Socio-Archeological Approach* (SWBAS, 9; Sheffield: Almond Press, 1991); Knauf, 'The Migration of the Script'; *idem*, 'War Biblisch-Hebräisch eine Sprache? Empirische Gesichtspunkte zur Annäherung an die Sprache der althebräischen Literatur', *ZAH* 3 (1990), pp. 11-23; H.M. Niemann, 'Stadt, Land und Herrschaft. Skizzen und Materialien zur Sozialgeschichte im monarchischen Israel' (B-dissertation, Rostock, 1990).

3. A primary example is provided by Tel Dan, where LB/Iron I destruction levels are imagined rather than evidenced; see H.M. Niemann, *Die Daniten. Studien zur Geschichte eines altisraelitischen Stammes* (Göttingen: Vandenhoeck & Ruprecht, 1985), p. 261 on the one hand and the reviews of V. Fritz (*TRev* 81 [1985], pp. 460-62) and E.A. Knauf (*ZDPV* 101 [1985], pp. 183-87) on the other.

4. Although pottery producers (like producers of other goods) may apply production and decoration techniques that are specific for an individual ethnic group or may cater to the taste of such a group (K.A. Kamp and N. Yoffee, 'Ethnicity in

In consequence, archaeology is either forced by the literature-oriented historian to say things that archaeology cannot say, which seems to have been the basic attitude of the 'Albright school' (and which has received its fair amount of criticism);[1] or, archaeology is simply ignored by these historians, or at least most of its potential contribution to history, as was the case in the scholarly tradition inaugurated by Alt and Noth.[2]

Ancient Western Asia During the Early Second Millennium BC', *BASOR* 237 [1980], pp. 85-104; Knauf, *Midian*, pp. 17-21), the production and distribution of any artifact is basically an economic phenomenon that has little political significance (even in Europe's darkest period, 1870–1945, there was Wedgewood and Sèvres in German households and collections and Meissen porcelain in London and Paris). Cf. P.J. Parr, 'Pottery, People and Politics', in *Archaeology in the Levant. Essays in Honor of K. Kenyon* (Warminster: Aris & Philipps, 1978), pp. 202-209; B. Mershen, 'Recent Hand-Made Pottery from Northern Jordan', *Berytus* 33 (1985), pp. 75-87.

1. For critical assessments of the Albrightian approach, see M. Noth, 'Grundsätzliches zur geschichtlichen Deutung archäologischer Befunde auf dem Boden Palästinas', *PJ* 34 (1938), pp. 7-22; idem, 'Der Beitrag der Archäologie zur Geschichte Israels', *Congress Volume Oxford 1959* (VTSup 7; ed. G.W. Anderson *et al.*; Leiden: Brill, 1960), pp. 262-82; M. Weippert, *Die Landnahme der israelitischen Stämme in der neueren wissenschaftlichen Diskussion. Ein kritischer Bericht* (FRLANT, 92; Göttingen: Vandenhoeck & Ruprecht, 1967), pp. 123-39; J.M. Miller, 'Approaches to the Bible through History and Archaeology: Biblical History as a Discipline', *BA* 45 (1982), pp. 211-16; N.A. Silberman, Review of *The Scholarship of William Foxwell Albright*, ed. G.W. Van Beek, *BA* 52 (1989), p. 231.

2. Although A. Alt can be credited with having inaugurated the study of ancient Israel's history as a process founded on a basically valid interpretation of settlement patterns—and thus, on archaeology—in the specific form of his 'Landnahme' theory, his pupils were content to dogmatize his (wrong) conclusions instead of extending his research strategy into fields other than the prehistory of Israel. (Alt's lasting achievement is duly emphasized by I. Finkelstein [*Settlement*]). Noth's defense against the charge of not using archaeological evidence to its full extent ('Beitrag', p. 272 n. 17) betrays a serious misapprehension of what archaeology can be and can do. On the other hand, I would not say that Albright and Bright used archaeology to its full extent either, but they undoubtedly used more of it. As long as history is primarily based on texts and as long as the historian tries to relate archaeological results to his texts, only a very small segment of the archaeological data can be processed (cf. Noth, 'Deutung', p. 8). Instead of being regarded as a source in its own right, archaeology is relegated to the status of an appendix of illustrations to a history that has been established along the lines of ancient narrative (*ibid.*, p. 7).

If the sources—or a whole category of primary documentation, that is, the material cultural remains—do not give reasonable answers, one probably has asked the wrong questions. Archaeology's inability to answer the traditional questions of historians has lead to the slander of 'archaeology's silence', which consciously or unconsciously tries to characterize the archaeologist's claim to 'read' sherds and to 'interpret' soil layer sequences as a suspicious modern variety of charlatanry. Actually, the archaeological evidence is no more silent than the Torah is to somebody who cannot read Hebrew. In both cases, you either undergo training in which you are provided with a theoretical background that allows you to make sense out of your source— disputable sense, of course—or you are at the mercy of those who did.

The disregard for nontextual sources and, accordingly, the failure to train one's eye as thoroughly in 'reading' pictures, configurations of material remains, and landscapes, together with the unquestioned expectation that our doctoral candidates be trained in a variety of European and Near Eastern languages, can be traced back to an influential 'Puritan' strain in the Judeo-Christian heritage and, hence, in western intellectual culture. How detrimental an inability to think in pictures has been for the understanding of the Hebrew Bible has now amply been demonstrated by Othmar Keel, although his insights are still far from being common knowledge.[1]

Needless to say, even if archaeological evidence is processed, it is processed only as a poor substitute for the texts that we are lacking and is immediately abandoned by historians as soon as they have, or assume they have, written sources (Noth's discussion of the impact of archaeology on biblical study does not contain a single instance that refers to Israel's history after 1000 BCE). How histories (other than prehistories) can differ according to whether archaeology or the historical tradition provides the reconstruction's point of departure can easily be illustrated by the case of Edomite history; contrast I. Willi-Plein, 'Genesis 27 als Rebekkageschichte. Zu einem historigraphischen Kunstgriff der biblischen Vätergeschichte', *TZ* 45 (1989), pp. 315-34, esp. p. 318 with E.A. Knauf, 'Supplementa Ismaelitica 13. Edom und Arabien', *BN* 45 (1988), pp. 62-81.

1. See, e.g., O. Keel, 'Grundsätzliches zum Neumondemblem zwischen den Bäumen', *BN* 6 (1978), pp. 40-55; *idem, Jahwes Entgegnung an Ijob. Eine Deutung von Ijob 38-41 vor dem Hintergrund der zeitgenösischen Bildkunst* (Göttingen: Vandenhoeck & Ruprecht, 1978); *idem, Das Böcklein in der Milch seiner Mutter und Verwandtes. Im Lichte eines altorientalischen Bildmotivs* (OBO, 33; Göttingen: Vandenhoeck & Ruprecht, 1980); *idem*, 'Bildträger aus Palästina/Israel und die besondere Bedeutung der Miniaturkunst', in *Studien zu den*

There is yet another reason why archaeology has been condemned to silence for so long. As long as history is restricted to political history, the history of human decisions and events, archaeology is mute indeed. Pots do not betray the passport information concerning their producers and users; ruins may provide clues for the origin of their present state (earthquake, an accidental fire, dilapidation due to neglect, warfare), but they seldom tell who did it. Thanks to a growing interest in social and economic history that started at the end of the last century in response to the challenge of Marxism,[1] and thanks even more to Lucien Febvre, Fernand Braudel and the Annales-school,[2] a growing number of historians have become aware of another history beyond the history of kings, states, and nations: the history of everyday life, the anonymous history, the history of long-term change in human life and society. For those interested in this kind of history, it is rather the historiographical heritage of the ancient world that has become mute.

Following Fernand Braudel,[3] we have to distinguish levels of his-

Stempelsiegeln aus Palästina/Israel (OBO, 67: ed. O. Keel and S. Schroer; Göttingen: Vandenhoeck & Ruprecht, 1985), pp. 26-38.

1.   Cf. H. Schleier, 'Der Kulturhistoriker Karl Lamprecht, der "Methodenstreit" und die Folgen', in *Karl Lamprecht—Alternative zu Ranke*, pp. 7-37.

2.   When, in 1929, Lucien Febvre and Marc Bloch started to publish the *Annales. Economies—Sociétés—Civilisations* (as they were finally called), history had become a social (and political) science with open borders to geography, sociology, anthropology, and archaeology: cf. I. Wallerstein, *The Capitalist World-Economy* (Cambridge: Cambridge University Press, 1979), pp. vii-xii. In Germany, where the ideology of 'interpreting humanities' (*verstehende Geisteswissenschaften*) versus 'measuring and counting sciences' (*quantifizierende Naturwissenschaften*) still prevails, the new concept's radicality was domesticated by adding 'economic history' or 'empirical historical sociology' in the margin of the historical profession; cf. M. Erbe, *Zur neueren französischen Sozialgeschichtsforschung. Die Gruppe um die 'Annales'* (Erträge der Forschung, 110; Darmstadt: Wissenschaftliche Buchgesellschaft, 1979); H. Best and H. Schröder, 'Quantitative historische Sozialforschung', in *Historische Methode. Theorie der Geschichte*, V (ed. C. Meier and J. Rüsten; Munich: Deutscher Taschenbuch Verlag, 1988), pp. 235-66.

3.   Braudel's method is best elucidated (better, in my opinion, than in his theoretical contributions) by its application to a great theme: F. Braudel, *The Mediterranean and the Mediterranean World in the Age of Philip II* (2 vols.; London: Collins, 1972). In addition, this book ought to be required reading for anybody interested in any part of the history of Palestine, a country that happens to be a part of

torical analysis that work with different sets of data and use different research strategies and are due, to a certain extent, to different theoretical perceptions of history.

On the first and basic level, history presents itself as the process of humanity's social, political, economical and technical evolution. Under 'history as a process' I suggest the inclusion of both the 'structures', Braudel's long-term level, and the 'conjunctures', Braudel's medium-term level. From the point of view of the individual who acts, both 'structures' and 'conjunctures' describe a state of the world beyond the individual's reach, changing in terms that far surpass one human's lifetime and experience. But accumulated actions of individual persons can create 'structures' in the course of the millennia. History as a process describes our common fate beyond the influence of conscious decision-making. It describes, for example, the humanly influenced nature of the Sahara that is not so much the product of climatic change as it is the product of overgrazing.[1] No individual ever said 'Let's turn North Africa into a vast desert'; however, responsibility comes with the possibility of knowledge. No individual human being ever

the Mediterranean world, a fact frequently forgotten by those who have arrived at Jerusalem without paying due respect to Athens and Rome. Needless to say, Braudel's *Méditerranée*, the Annales-school's *ouvre emblématique*, has not yet been received in Germany; in the best Hegelian manner ('If the facts contradict my theory, I feel sorry for the facts'), H. Lutz ('Braudels *La Méditerranée*. Zur Problematik eines Modellanspruchs', in *Formen der Geschichtsschreibung. Theorie der Geschichte*, IV [ed. R. Koselleck *et al.*; Munich: Deutscher Taschenbuch Verlag, 1982], pp. 320-51) is able to argue that Braudel is not that important after all, especially since his book suffers from shortcomings that became obvious when some of Braudel's results were surpassed by the work of his pupils. (Newton, then, was a mediocre physicist because he did not develop Einstein's theories of relativity, and Einstein really is overestimated because one day there will be a Zweistein who, like every gifted student is expected to do, may improve the work of his predecessors).

1. Cf. K.H. Striedter, *Felsbilder der Sahara* (Munich: Prestel, 1984), pp. 9-61; W. Schenkel, *Die altägyptische Suffixkonjugation* (Ägyptologische Abhandlungen, 32; Wiesbaden: Otto Harrassowitz, 1975), pp. 69-71; H.J. Pachur and H.-P. Röper, 'The Libyan (Western) Desert and Northern Sudan during the Late Pleistocene and Holocene', *Berliner Geographische Abhandlungen* 50 (1984), pp. 249-84. Similarly, overgrazing in the neolithic period accounts for the present state of the flint desert of Jordan; cf. A.N. Garrard *et al.*, 'Prehistoric Environment and Settlement in the Azraq Basin: an Interim Report on the 1985 Excavation Season', *Levant* 19 (1987), pp. 5-25, esp. p. 7.

decided to pollute the air or to overpopulate our planet. Still, this is what happened and what we now have to face.

Processual history is nothing but an extension of natural history into the specific realm of *homo sapiens*, whose *sapientia* operates on only a very restricted segment of what this species actually does and effects. Far from determining human history past and present, processual (or structural) history elucidates the conditions and limitations, the possibilities and impossibilities under and among which the people of the past had to live and had to make their decisions. People always have choices—but which choices did they actually have?

Processual (or structural) history cannot do without archaeology. In order to describe the functioning of any ancient society and in order to trace processes that transformed past societies, we need representative, quantitative date that are firmly positioned in space and time. We need to know the shape of ordinary life, not of the extraordinary, which by definition is regarded as an 'event' and goes into the narrative sources.[1] It is on the processual level that we may expect answers to the questions of Israel's origin, the origin of its religion, and the emergence, rise and fall of Israelite states. Whatever the achievements of some individuals in these processes were (and I am far from denying that such individual achievements can be seen operating), there are structural reasons for their success or the reception of their ideas. Structures may explain why Saul became the first Israelite king (whatever 'being king' meant then and there), not Jerubbaal or Abimelech; why the Roman empire could survive a Caligula, a Nero and an Elagabal, whereas the kingdom of Judah did not survive Zedekiah's revolt and Gedaliah's assassination.[2] If a non-archaeologist may be

---

1.   The structures, the conditions of ordinary life, and their gradual changes are attested in the archaeological record (and in the account books), whereas narrative accounts focus on the events, the extraordinary by definition. Disregard of this distinction and of what specific sources can and cannot say turns the discussion between S.Th. Parker ('Peasants, Pastoralists, and *Pax Romana*: A Different View', *BASOR* 265 [1987], pp. 35-51) and E.B. Banning ('Peasants, Pastoralists and *Pax Romana*: Mutualism in the Southern Highlands of Jordan', *BASOR* 261 [1986], pp. 25-50; and 'De Bello Paceque: A Reply to Parker', *BASOR* 265 [1987], pp. 52-54) into a series of unconnected monologues; cf. also P. Mayerson, 'Saracens and Romans: Micro-Macro-Relationships', *BASOR* 274 (1989), pp. 71-79.

2.   As J.M. Miller and J.H. Hayes (*A History of Ancient Israel and Judah* [Philadelphia: Westminster Press, 1986], pp. 421-26) have convincingly argued,

allowed this remark, I should like to stress that in order to provide the answers that can duly be expected from archaeology, Palestinian archaeology still has to learn to spell its theories within the alphabet of cultural time and to rid itself of the eggshells of political or historical time imposed on it by its 'biblical' beginnings.[1] On the level of process, there is no boundary between history, prehistory, and natural history.

Historical (or political) time works on the level of history seen as a chain of events, of human (or superhuman) actions and decisions. Historical time only exists within the sphere of writing, as history as a chain of events only exists within the broader category of narrative. As the construction of any chain of events is based on a collective or individual decision about what is meaningful and relevant, the eventual level of history is textual by nature. Meaning is not an attribute of

Gedaliah ben Ahikam was the last king of Judah.

1.   In a misguided attempt to cater to the traditional historian, surprisingly many archaeologists use nonsensical *political* definitions for periods of *cultural* history as, e.g., 'Iron II C = 722–586 BCE' or 'Early Byzantine I = 324–363' (what possible impact could the emperors' change of religion have on pottery production in rural Palestine?). An Edomite *polity* is attested from the late 9th century BCE until 552 BCE (cf. above); a specifically Edomite *pottery* was probably produced from the 7th century BCE through the 5th century (cf. S. Hart, 'Some Preliminary Thoughts on Settlement in Southern Jordan', *Levant* 18 [1986], pp. 51-58). Thus, one could define 'Iron II C' for the region south of Wadi al-Hasa as corresponding roughly to 700–450 BCE, a cultural definition that demonstrates to the political historian that a new state does not immediately give rise to a new civilisation, nor does its final demise imply the civilisation's immediate disappearance. For the problem of cultural versus political chronology (or 'texts' versus 'archaeology', again), see A.E. Glock, 'Texts and Archaeology at Tell Ta'annek', *Berytus* 31 (1983), pp. 57-66; C.J. Lenzen and E.A. Knauf, 'Beit Ras/Capitolias. A Preliminary Evaluation of the Archaeological and Textual Evidence', *Syria* 64 (1987), pp. 21-46, esp. p. 41 n. 89; E.A. Knauf and C.J. Lenzen, 'Edomite Copper Industry', in *Studies in the History and Archaeology of Jordan*, III (ed. A. Hadidi; Amman: Department of Antiquities, 1987), pp. 83-88, esp. pp. 86-87; D.J. Whitcomb, 'Khirbet al-Mafjar Reconsidered: The Ceramic Evidence', *BASOR* 271 (1988), pp. 51-67; H. Weippert, *Palästina in vorhellenistischer Zeit. Handbuch der Archäologie: Vorderasien*, II.1 (Munich: Beck, 1988), pp. 25-32. The momentum that the 'new archaeology' movement gave to the archaeology of Palestine towards finding words (theories, research programs, hypotheses) to 'say its own thing' can only be gratefully acknowledged; cf. W.G. Dever, 'Retrospects and Prospects in Syro-Palestinian Archaeology', *BA* 45 (1982), pp. 103-107.

'things as they are'; meaning is attributed to certain things by the human mind that perceives meaning by creating it. Basically, meaning exists in a world constituted by texts, both written and oral, conscious and subconscious, explicit and implicit. The constitution of 'events' as a selection of the meaningful from among the impenetrable chaos of 'what actually is happening' starts on the level of the written sources, if not before, and extends into their reorganization by the historian: Alexander's killing of Kleitos is an event, while a Macedonian soldier's 'killing' of six jugs of wine is not (rather, it is a universal structure). On the level of events, history cannot do without written sources and the information that they provide about actors, places and time. Ranke still deserves credit for directing the historian's attention to those texts that were produced in the course of the events as they were happening (the primary sources) and luring them away from those texts that were produced after the events in an attempt to clarify for future generations how things were thought to have happened (the secondary, tertiary, and quarternary sources).[1]

Sadly, a large segment of present biblical historiography still lives in a pre-Ranke world and gives improper weight to the Hebrew Bible as a historical source for everything that happened before the 7th century BCE, neglecting the primary sources, whose number is already vast and steadily increasing.[2] For this period, the Bible is a secondary

---

1.   Ancient Near Eastern historiography (including biblical and early Islamic historiography) is not concerned with what actually had happened. Rather, it is interested in stating what should have happened in order to construct a 'correct' world; cf. H.J. Nissen, *Grundzüge einer Geschichte der Frühzeit des Vorderen Orients* (Grundzüge, 52; Darmstadt: Wissenschaftliche Buchgesellschaft, 1983), pp. 4-5; Knauf, *Ismael*, pp. 96-99; *idem, Midian*, pp. 147-71; P. Crone, *Meccan Trade and the Rise of Islam* (Oxford: Basil Blackwell, 1987), pp. 203-30.

2.   Is it possible and desirable to write a history of ancient Israel/Palestine without any regard for the Bible? It is probably possible—and worth a try—although it will be very hard to eliminate from the back of the historian's mind what is common knowledge in the Western culture—the biblical tradition. It is hardly desirable (except for the delineation of evidence that can by no sensible means be disputed to exist; 'sensible means', because there will always be some Dänikens and Salibis around, and 'disputed to exist', since the impact and significance of every piece of evidence that happened to exist always is disputable). It is not desirable because a literary corpus like the Bible is in itself a primary source for the intellectual life, if nothing else, of the period which produced it. Of course, primary dated sources will always take precedence over secondary sources that can be dated with some effort only. In

source at best.[1] At the same time, no history of events can claim to represent 'what actually happened'. It can only claim to preserve what its author or authors regarded worthy of remembrance. For all its inherent fallacies, its obvious subjectivism, its biased, sometimes myopic selection of the material that is processed, we cannot totally abandon the history of events for the scientific and objective history of processes if we intend to study history as human history and if we maintain that there is some basic difference between human beings and wolves. Even on the level of events, history remains inside the wider field of anthropology: it broadens our perception of the human nature, its potential as well as its limitations, by confronting us with past organizations of humanity. Only on the level of events can we talk about human decisions and their consequences, folly and punishment. As much as the human fate in the past as in the present was and is shaped by conditions caused by mankind without anybody's intent, so much does an appropriate understanding of past human actions and their consequences require a dialogue between the processual and the eventual level of analysis.

On the level of the chain of events, history becomes narrative. On that level, there is no boundary between story and history. *Si non e vero, e bene trovato.* In his first methodological principle, Albright was right: without 'external evidence', that is, evidence from outside the narrative or the complex of narratives that we intend to analyze historically, we can never decide (beyond statements of personal taste or beliefs which are epistemologically quite irrelevant) whether a

the example of the treatment of Gedaliah by Miller and Hayes, this is exactly what they did (cf. above). In practice, Miller and Hayes go well beyond their goal to provide a historical companion to the Bible (cf. J.M. Miller, 'In Defense of Writing a History of Israel', *JSOT* 39 [1987], pp. 53-57)—which still could and would be a useful book, but not a history of ancient Israel and Judah.

1.   The Hebrew Bible may contain authentic documents (lists of tribes, places and officials) that are as early as the 9th century BCE and some poetry (Exod. 15.21; Num. 21.14-15; Judg. 5) that may even be older. Narratives containing eyewitness reports do not commence, as far as I see, before the end of the 8th century. But to identify and retrieve these documents, theoretical reconstructions concerning the growth of a literary tradition that, according to orthography and grammar, was not finalized before the 5th/4th centuries BCE (cf. above) are required. We simply do not have the documents; all we can do is in some cases reasonably assume that we may have copies of copies.

story relates to the past real world or is just well invented (it is another question, of course, if all the 'external evidence' ever adduced actually holds water).[1] Here is the third level of historical analysis that ought to be considered in addition to Braudel's levels: narrative. The consideration of narrative in historical studies has a self-critical aspect in addition to its source-critical aspects. A narrative is what the historian finally produces as long as it is written in the preterit. Language wisely makes no difference between the textual mode of history and the mode of story: what is no longer real because it is past is told in the same mode as that which is not real because it is imagined.[2]

As the meaning of a narrative is yet different from the meaning of its elements, historical narrative forms a separate level of inquiry. As a narrative construct, history adopts purpose and intent. On the narrative level, the hidden or open agenda of the historian, ancient and modern, can be detected. As meaning, purpose and intent are inherent in the text and not in the data, narrative history is always in danger of becoming myth: a construct of nonevents, texts generated in response

1.   Albright's insight that stories can only be associated with history if they provide clues that link them to texts or artifacts firmly anchored in the time-space universe led him to claim such clues where there are actually none, as Noth ('Beitrag', p. 270 n. 15) pointed out. Because he did not have the 'external evidence' that he would have liked to have had, Noth (and his followers) relied heavily on his reconstruction of Israel's literary and ideological history—a reconstruction that can, and in the recent past has been, easily falsified by adducing linguistic and anthropological data (cf. Knauf, *Ismael*, pp. 17-45, 140-43). As biblical historians, we need external evidence and usually do not have enough. In consequence, we should stick to statements and theories that can be tested by material not yet excavated and abstain from statements that, from an empirical point of view, are neither wrong nor true because they cannot be tested.

2.   For the 'narrative mode' as opposed to the 'real world mode', see H. Weinrich, *Tempus. Besprochene und erzählte Welt* (2nd rev. edn; Stuttgart: Kohlhammer, 1971). Although the 'narrative mode' is indicated by more than just verbal forms (*pace* Weinrich), in at least those Semitic and Indo-European languages that I am able to read, the 'world of the narrative' and the 'world of the past' coincide linguistically. I would be surprised if this rule did not apply to Chinese, Tamil and Navajo too. It is only from our knowledge of controlling data—i.e., external evidence such as the biographical background of the author and his use of sources—that we classify Stefan Heym's *King David Report* as fiction, and Edward Gibbon's *Decline and Fall of the Roman Empire* as an attempt to write history (both are great literature though—and stimulating, if somewhat biased attempts in historiography at the same time).

to other texts that still can be meaningful, but cannot claim to be rooted in real space and time.[1] Although the construct of a past real world is just one theoretical construct among many others, it is the construct produced by objective history as characterized above (i.e. the historical world is constructed in accordance with our construction of present reality). If history is understood as the historical dimension of anthropology, distinguishing between what can and what cannot be supposed really to have happened becomes quite relevant. Before we can proceed from the narrative level on which all ancient historiography came down to us to the level of events or even processes, there must always be a critical deconstruction of the narrative.[2] To leap from narrative to archaeology and back again is the best way to produce a pseudohistory of nonevents.[3] C.N. Parkinson's genial location

---

1. The biblical Balaam, for example, is the result of a long literary history without any regard for 'historical facts' ('facts' according to present perceptions of factuality). This history's extrabiblical point of departure is now circumscribed by the Deir 'Alla plaster inscriptions; significantly, no 'traditio-historical' reconstruction of Balaam's origins based on the biblical texts had ever lead to Gilead. Cf. for the Balaam 'traditions', H. Donner, 'Balaam pseudopropheta', in *Beiträge zur alttestamentlichen Theologie: Festschrift W. Zimmerli zum 70. Geburtstag* (ed. H. Donner *et al.*; Göttingen: Vandenhoeck & Ruprecht, 1977), pp. 112-23; Knauf, *Midian*, pp. 161-67; S. Timm, *Moab zwischen den Mächten. Studien zu historischen Denkmälern und Texten* (ÄAT, 17; Wiesbaden: Otto Harrassowitz, 1989), pp. 97-157. Cf. further for 'fiction' and 'historical fiction' in the Hebrew Bible, H. Niehr, *Rechtsprechung in Israel. Untersuchungen zur Geschichte der Gerichtsorganisation in Israel* (SBS, 130; Stuttgart: Katholisches Bibelwerk, 1987), pp. 13-17, 118-27.

2. Thus I cannot disagree with Noth's criticism of Albright's methodology ('Beitrag', p. 270 n. 15). One should not forget, however, that Noth and his school had and still have their own favorite points at which they leap from a critical analysis of the texts to a historical reality that is supposed to correspond to the texts' favorite concepts, thus creating a number of modern scholastic myths that are still influential: the settlement by land-hungry nomads, a premonarchic Israelite nation, pre-exilic or even premonarchic mono- or henotheism, etc.

3. According to R.G. Boling (*The Early Biblical Community in Transjordan*, pp. 41-52), Heshbon must be looked for somewhere else because King Sihon does not show up in the archaeological record at Tell Ḥisbân. As J.M. Miller ('Site Identification: A Problem Area in Contemporary Biblical Scholarship', *ZDPV* 99 [1983], pp. 119-29, esp. pp. 122-25) has pointed out, this assumption is rather unlikely from the point of view of historical topography. For H.C. Schmitt ('Das Hesbonlied Num. 21,27aßb-30 und die Geschichte der Stadt Hesbon', *ZDPV* 104 [1988], pp. 26-43), Timm (*Moab*, pp. 62-96), and Knauf ('Hesbon, Sihons Stadt',

of Smallbridge Manor, Viscount Hornblower's estate, is historical topography at its best; it still cannot silence those who maintain that the first Viscount Hornblower is nothing but a piece of 20th century fiction.[1]

It is on the narrative level that the intentionality of any history becomes evident (including histories constructed objectively). Every history, critical or uncritical, is constructed from a present point of view with a present purpose to serve.[2] Objectively viewed, history neither justifies nor excuses anything: it is always our moral, ethical, or political system of thought that excuses, justifies, or accuses. Murderers are prosecuted in most societies; but definitions of what constitutes a murder that ought to be prosecuted vary widely. The objective fact of a person killing another person does not automatically induce the category of a murderer who has to be punished. Sometimes, it establishes the category of a hero who has to be decorated. The moral, ethical and political issues that underlie claims, justifications, and accusations have to be discussed. But they can be discussed more clearly if not disguised as 'historical rights' that, incidentally, do not appear in any catalogue of human rights.[3]

ZDPV 106 [1990] in print), there is no 'King Sihon' in the earliest biblical reference to 'Sihon's town' either.

1. Cf. C.N. Parkinson, *The Life and Times of Horatio Hornblower* (London: Allen Sutton, 1970), Appendix IV.

2. One of the main uses of history is to construct ethnic identity, and ethnic identity is never constructed without political purpose. Cf. K.W. Whitelam, 'Israel's Traditions of Origin: Reclaiming the Land', *JSOT* 44 (1989), pp. 19-42. Some examples from the contemporary Near East can be seen among minor tribes of southern Jordan who are at present increasingly successful in claiming descent from the Huweitat tribe, politically and economically the most powerful tribe in the area, which in turn claims much more prestigious origins than are reconcilable with the documented history of the area; cf. Knauf, *Midian*, pp. 3 n. 13, 33 n. 168; R. Bocco and A. Ohanessian-Charpin, 'A propos du mythe de fondation de la tribu bédouine des Huwaytât', in *Mémoire de soie. Costumes et parures de Palestine et de Jordanie* (ed. I. Abback and J. Hannoyer; Paris: EDIFRA, 1988), pp. 72-81. According to the informants' actual interest, history is as variable and adaptable as is ethnicity; cf. K. Hackstein, *Ethnizität und Situation. Garas—eine vorderorientalische Kleinstadt* (BTAVO B, 94; Wiesbaden: Reichert, 1989), pp. 36-50.

3. The 'argument from history' is still prevalent among rightist German groups who claim the western part of the present Polish Republic as 'German' territory because these territories once belonged to German states. Significantly, this 'argu-

Excursus: History, Archaeology and Biblical Studies

Within the theoretical framework presented above, a question of long standing evaporates: how does archaeology relate to biblical studies? I feel sorry for the streams of ink that have been spilled on this question, and quite in vain (well, better ink spilled than blood). Within the traditional concept of history where the historian retells old tales, they cannot relate to each other.[1] Once history is understood as the product of the historian, they do not 'relate' either, at least no more than flour relates to milk in a bakery. Historians need primary sources and have to look for them. They must take what they can find, be it written or unwritten.

Of course, the insistence on primary sources largely disqualifies the Bible as a historical source—at least for the time before it was canonized (for the time after canonization, the historical significance of the Bible, i.e. its cultural impact, can hardly be overestimated). The Bible is a secondary source at best, even for those centuries that are covered by contemporary biblical authors like Jeremiah and Qoheleth (it still is disputed and takes some theoretical effort to attribute texts in Jeremiah to the first half of the 6th century BCE and the bulk of Qoheleth to the 3rd century BCE). Even as a secondary source, the Bible still is an important historical source for the social, religious and literary history of the ancient Near East in the first millennium BCE, but it is only a historical source in the hands of a historian. This,

---

ment from history' is highly selective: it leaves the reasons why the Polish borders now are where they are out of its focus. There is no question that criminal acts in the past, be they committed by states or individuals in the service of states, are to be brought to justice and claims by the victims enacted. But do states or nations have any rights other than those derived from the inalienable human rights of the individual persons whom they represent? This is probably the most virulent open question in international law. There is no question that if states and nations would abandon the 'argument from history' and justify their existence by a functioning democracy and an impeccable human rights record (i.e. by the human rights of the citizens whom they serve), we would live in a world with significantly more peace, both inside and between states.

1. The pitfalls of relating stones, dirt, and sherds to texts (instead of relating both to the hypothetical past world whose remnants they are) are obvious in every treatment of the 'Bible and archaeology' question from the biblicist's point of view; cf. in addition to the articles by M. Noth the recent essay by C. Frevel, '"Dies ist der Ort, von dem geschrieben steht..." Zum Verhältnis von Bibelwissenschaft und Palästinaarchäologie', *BN* 77 (1989), pp. 35-89.

however, does not make every biblical scholar a historian.[1]

Traditionally, history, especially ancient history, has been institutionally linked (and still is in continental Europe) with philology instead of the human sciences. That fact can be held responsible for the still prevalent understanding of history in central Europe as a special aspect of interpreting ancient texts, leading to the philologists' claim to historical competence and to the repeated statement that it is impossible to write the history of ancient people—or past centuries—who did not write their own history or whose historiography has been lost.[2] The fear of venturing out on the ocean of facts with nothing but

---

1. I assume that the average central European biblicist's claim to be—by profession—a historian in addition to being a student of literature and a theologian lies behind the criticism that I would deny any historical importance to the Bible (e.g. H.-J. Fabry, 'Erst die Erstgeburt, dann der Segen. Eine Nachfrage zu Gen 27, 1-45', in *Vom Sinai zum Horeb. Situationen alttestamentlicher Glaubensgeschichte* [ed. F.L. Hossfeld; Würzburg: Echter Verlag, 1989], pp. 51-72, esp. pp. 67, 72). I do not, as should be evident from the biblical texts that I have tried to interpret historically in the course of the last decade. However, I maintain that secondary sources cannot compete with primary evidence, that our theoretical concept of 'history' should have advanced beyond concepts of the first millennium BCE, and that exegetical skills are not enough to make a historian. I also assume that biblicists' claims to historical competence ultimately derive from Martin Luther's hermeneutical claim that the historical sense of the Bible is its theological sense. Regardless of whether this is a tenable theological position, it is not a position that a 20th-century historian can take, as our perception of 'history' significantly deviates from pre-enlightenment concepts.

2. The claim that one cannot write ancient history without ancient narrative sources, inherited from the days when history was one of the by-products of philology, can still be found in W. Huss, *Geschichte der Karthager* (Handbuch der Altertumswissenschaft, III.8; Munich: Beck, 1985), p. xi; H. Donner, *Geschichte des Volkes Israel und seiner Nachbarn in Grundzügen. II. Von der Königszeit bis zu Alexander dem Grossen. Mit einem Ausblick auf die Geschichte des Judentums bis Bar Kochba* (Göttingen: Vandenhoeck & Ruprecht, 1986), p. 434: 'Der Historiker, der gar keine unmittelbaren literarischen Quellen zur Verfügung hat, kann nicht Geschichte schreiben'. Donner made this remark in regard of the 'dark 4th century BCE'; for that period, contrast M.A. Dandamaev, *A Political History of the Achaemenid Empire* (Leiden: Brill, 1989), pp. 270-313. I want to stress that both Huss and Donner wrote competent, readable, and partially innovative histories whose scope and content belies their methodological timidity. If we cannot reconstruct the history of ancient people whose historians never wrote their own histories, or whose historians' works are not transmitted, the ancient 'people without history' would forever remain without history. That's hardly fair, is it?

a directive (a research program) of one's own making is understandable—for then, nobody can be blamed in case of failure but the historians themselves. But again, to understand does not mean to excuse, and indeed it is the historian and not the sources that are to be held responsible for any shortcomings that may be produced in the process of constituting history. The widespread attitude of following the shorelines of tradition instead of the stars of anthropological theory is also operative in the production of histories that provide (sometimes excellent) collections and discussions of data—but no history.[1] Historians are requested to master their sources (hopefully, as many as possible), not to be their slaves. The chance of shipwreck is rather high close to the shores; on the high seas, on the other hand, you are more likely to drown if you fail.

History and the Student of the Bible

The attitude of the historian, who wants precise answers to precise questions, is diametrically opposed to the attitude of the exegete, who wants the texts to deliver their 'original', 'true', or 'real' (German: *eigentlich*) message (regardless of the problem whether the 'original' and the 'true' message are necessarily identical).[2] Insofar as any reconstructed 'original' message is nothing if not a historical hypothesis, it never can be identical with the 'original message' that the text had for its first audience. We can try to know something about this original audience, but we can never be it. History and exegesis, which today look worlds apart, turn out to be two sides of the same coin, and it undoubtedly would enhance the clarity of exegetical discussions if exegetes would cease to embellish their theories with the authority of

1. Examples of useful collections and discussions of data which nevertheless are not histories are provided by R. Giveon, *Les bédouins* [sic] *Shosou des documents égyptiens* (DMOA, 18; Leiden: Brill, 1971) (contrast M. Weippert, 'Semitische Nomaden des zweiten Jahrtausends', *Bib* 55 [1974], pp. 265-80, 427-33); I. Eph'al, *The Ancient Arabs. Nomads on the Borders of the Fertile Crescent, 9th–5th Centuries BC* (Jerusalem: Magnes Press, 1982) (contrast Knauf, *Ismael*, pp. 136-38); Bartlett, *Edom and the Edomites* (contrast Knauf, 'Edom und Arabien').

2. Cf. J. Barr, 'The Literal, the Allegorical, and Modern Biblical Scholarship', *JSOT* 44 (1989), pp. 3-17. Cf. also T.L. Thompson, *The Origin Traditions of Ancient Israel. I. The Literary Formation of Genesis and Exodus 1-23* (JSOTSup, 55; Sheffield: JSOT Press, 1987), pp. 11-40, 199-212.

the Bible—an authority that we all respect whenever it is relied upon
by religious people in the course of the exercise of their religion, but
which has no argumentative value when it comes to discussing
conflicting theories. Given the three-level complexity of history, it is
obvious that we have to know history—as much history as possible—
before we can interpret ancient texts historically. I do not think that
we have the choice to interpret an ancient text nonhistorically. By its
very nature of being ancient, the text is separated from our world by
a non-negotiable gap in space, time and human self-perception.
Therefore, history applies also to those modes of interpretation that
try to find the 'true' message of the text by subjecting it to a universal
structure-of-literature approach: no 'close reading' can leap across
that gap which, if nothing else, necessitates translation before interpretation, and no translation of ancient words can achieve its objective
without a thorough knowledge of the ancient world.[1] Of course, there
are conflicting theories about ancient Israel's world on the market, as
there always have been and always will be (as long as the principle of
intellectual freedom in an open society prevails). Some theories are
possibly right, some are definitely wrong (and still on the market and
sold in high quantities), but without any doubt the worst history to use
in biblical interpretation is the zero-history: the belief that we could
operate in biblical interpretation without a consciously formulated
(or chosen) historical theory. If the zero-history or non-historical
approach is chosen, the interpreter's uncontrolled fancy substitutes for
controlled knowledge (i.e., knowledge that could be criticized in
order to be improved) in every respect in which the problem of
historical distance emerges. That there are some human (and
cosmological) universals which continue through the centuries is, of
course, our common assumption in trying to interpret ancient texts;
but only historical knowledge can decide which characteristics were
shared by past populations with 'people like you and me' and which

---

1.   To translate Hebrew *mlk* as 'king' does not imply that such a person was
actually the head of a state. Jeremiah's *mlky h-'rb* certainly were mere tribal leaders,
as were *qynw. . .mlk qdr*, the dedicator of the Maskhûta-bowls (Knauf, *Ismael*,
p. 105) and the Qedarite 'kings' in Ashurbanipal's inscriptions (*ibid.*, pp. 106
n. 579, 157). Englishmen of the 18th century conferred the title of 'king' on native
American tribal leaders who did not represent state societies; cf. F. Moore, *A Voyage
to Georgia Begun in the Year 1735* (Brunswick, GA: Fort Frederica Association,
1983), p. 23.

were not.[1] Understandably, a growing number of biblical interpreters tries to bypass history now that biblical history requires the command of an ever-increasing number of nonbiblical sources; but again, to understand does not mean to excuse.

2. *Hosea in Historical Perspective*

The interpretive potential of historical criticism for biblical studies may now briefly be demonstrated by applying the three levels of historical analysis to the prophecy of Hosea. This attempt is based on the assumption that the book of Hosea, though in its present form the product of an editorial process that took place in Jerusalem and proceeded in various stages for more than two hundred years, is based on an Israelite (northern Hebrew) original draft that was completed, if not during the prophet's lifetime, then shortly thereafter.[2] More critical colleagues may regard an approach that accepts the presence of

1. Our default assumption is and has to be that all human beings are equal. Only empirically controlled research can elucidate in which respect they are not. (Quite obviously, the biblical authors did not share our opinions regarding the rights of women, children, slaves and aliens). To define culture-specific attitudes and behavioral modes for the ancient world is one of the main tasks of the historian. That, in some respects, ancient Hebrew thought was different from our way of thinking does not mean that modern scholars are allowed to supply their personal favorite deviation from rational thought for the 'biblical' attitude. For a criticism of that procedure, quite frequent among theologians, see J. Barr, *The Semantics of Biblical Language* (Oxford: Oxford University Press, 1961) and E. Koschmieder, *Die noetischen Grundlagen der Syntax* (Sitzungsberichte der Bayerischen Akademie der Wissenschaften, Philosophisch-historische Klasse, 1951, Heft 4; Munich: Beck, 1952). For viable ways to investigate the history of mentalities, the works of Philippe Ariès, Michel Foucault and their pupils provide outstanding examples. For the discussion of a gross example of 'pseudohistory by default', see D. Edelman, 'An Appraisal of Robert Alter's Approach', *Biblical Research* 31 (1986), pp. 19-25, esp. pp. 24-25.

2. Cf. for the redactional history of the book of Hosea I. Willi-Plein, *Vorformen der Schriftexegese innerhalb des Alten Testaments. Untersuchungen zum literarischen Werden der auf Amos, Hosea und Micha zurückgehenden Bücher im hebräischen Zwölfprophetenbuch* (BZAW, 123; Berlin: de Gruyter, 1971); G.A. Yee, *Composition and Tradition in the Book of Hosea. A Redaction Critical Investigation* (SBLDS, 102; Atlanta: Scholars Press, 1987). For macrohistorical and linguistic evidence that supports the assumption of Hoseanic texts in the book of Hosea, see Knauf, *Ismael*, pp. 35-36, 141 and 'War Biblisch-Hebräisch eine Sprache?'.

genuine sayings of the prophet in the book that carries his name as romantic and naïve,[1] but maybe that is what historians tend to be.

Hosea Constructs History

How history as a narrative construct works and how it obstructs historical research if not analyzed for what it is can be illustrated by Hosea's construction of 'Israel's prehistory in the desert'. Prior to Hosea, the relationship between Yahweh, Israel and the land was constituted by El's creation: 'When Elyon attributed their lots to the nations, divisioned the earthlings, then he decreed the limits of the nations according to the number of the sons of El. So it came to be that Yahweh's share is his people, Jacob the lot of his inheritance' (Deut. 32.8-9).[2] Thus, at least, ran the theology of pre-Josianic Jerusalem.[3] But in Hosea's view, Israel had perverted the cosmos of El's creation into utter chaos by rejecting its rightful god, Yahweh

---

1. The most 'negative' attitude towards our ability to retrieve texts from the late 8th century BCE in the book of Hosea is probably that of B.J. Diebner, 'Zur Funktion der kanonischen Textsammlung im Judentum der vorchristlichen Zeit. Gedanken zu einer Kanon-Hermeneutik', *DBAT* 22 (1985), pp. 58-73; *idem*, 'Überlegungen zum 'Brief de Elia' (2 Chr. 21, 12-15' *DBAT* 23-24 (1987), p. 94 n. 1.

2. According to the Septuagint. The Hebrew text has 'sons of Israel', an interpretation of Gen. 12.1-3 as seen from the diaspora experience. For the relevance and significance of Deut. 32.8-9 for the reconstruction of pre-exilic Israelite polytheism, see M. Weippert, 'Synkretismus und Monotheismus. Religionsinterne Konfliktbewältigung im Alten Israel', in *Kultur und Konflikt* (ed. J. Assmann: Frankfurt: Suhrkamp, 1990, in print).

3. The Jerusalemite pantheon, which is attested in Deut. 32.8-9 and which was restructured rather than abolished by Josiah (cf. L.K. Handy, 'A Realignment in Heaven: An Investigation into the Ideology of the Josianic Reform' [PhD dissertation, University of Chicago, 1987]), was established by Solomon when he introduced Yahweh into the Jebusite temple of El, Elyon and Elqōnē'arṣ (cf. 1 Kgs 1.12-13 according to the Septuagint and my forthcoming 'King Solomon's Copper Supply'). The god Elqōnē'arṣ is still attested on an ostracon from the 7th century BCE (cf. Knauf, 'Yahwe', *VT* 34 [1984], p. 470 n. 11). Jeremiah is the first prophet who preached Yahweh as a creator god; cf. H. Weippert, *Schöpfer des Himmels und der Erde* (SBS, 102; Stuttgart: Katholisches Bibelwerk, 1981). He also is the first monotheist among the prophets (Jer. 2.11). As far as I can see, there are no Israelite (as opposed to Judean or Jerusalemite) creation myths preserved in the Hebrew Bible. In the unquestionably Israelite text Judg. 5.4-5, Yahweh is a storm and weather god (as in 1 Kgs 8.12); thus, he is not a god of the El type.

(Hos. 4.3; 4.11; 9.16; 10.1-8; 13.15). In order to maintain hope for the re-emergence of order, it became necessary for Yahweh to establish his relationship with Israel outside the cosmos, which had proven defilable and corruptible, and to date the relationship prior to the history of Israel's corruption. Elaborating on the tradition that constituted Israel's self-perception after Yahweh became its god, 'Yahweh has lead Israel out of Egypt', Hosea chose the desert for Yahweh's adoption of Israel before Israel adopted him because the desert was the paradigmatic chaos, the noncosmos, to the ancients (2.4-17; 9.10).[1] A Yahweh who had sustained Israel in the chaos would be able to sustain it further in the corrupted cosmos of the land; at the same time, Hosea created a prehistory to Israel's corrupt (and continuing) history whose defilement was beyond the abilities of his and future generations. A history that has ended in failure is to be repeated: Israel, being sent back to Egypt, is undone in order to be recreated by its god (7.16; 8.13; 9.6, 17; 11.1-11). To undo history in order to redo it is inconceivable within our concepts of human individuality and singularity, but the thought is in accordance with Hosea's cosmological understanding of human deeds and their repercussions. The assumption that history can be redone underlies much, if not most of biblical historiography and characterizes the historical narrative not as an enumeration of facts, but as a program that is hoped to be implemented in the future because it is believed to have been accomplished in the past. It is not necessary to go beyond Hosea's mind to find a reason or a justification for Hosea's construct; therefore, it is not methodologically legitimate: *entia non sunt multiplicanda praeter necessitatem*.[2] Only by projecting the reception and elaboration of

---

1. Cf. S. Talmon, 'The "Desert Motif" in the Bible and in Qumran Literature', in *Biblical Motifs* (ed. A. Altmann; Cambridge, MA: Harvard University Press, 1966), pp. 31-63; E.A. Knauf, 'Hiobs Heimat', *Die Welt des Orients* 19 (1988), pp. 65-83, esp. pp. 69-72.

2. The narrative traditions concerning 'Israel in the desert' are post-Hoseanic. Cf. E. Zenger, *Israel am Sinai. Analysen und Interpretationen zu Exodus 17-34* (Altenberge: CIS, 1982). The concept of 'Israel in the desert' could easily develop once the Exodus tradition stating that 'Yahweh has brought us out of (the dominion of) Egypt' was understood to presuppose the one-time presence of Israel in Egypt (thus Amos 9.7)—an understanding that was hardly shared by the majority of early Israelites (cf. Knauf, *Midian*, pp. 106-10). That Yahweh himself was a desert god is not as evident as it is believed to be in the Alt school. Even if 'the one of Sinai'

Hosea's concept within the Hebrew Bible into 'traditions' and finally into a 'historical fact' of which Hosea is believed to have been aware is it still possible for central European mainstream scholarship to justify the assumption of Israel's 'nomadic origins' by a hypothesized consensus of biblical tradition about these origins.[1]

Hosea and the Events of his Time

For those of us who look for historical facts in the writings of Hosea, an awareness of differences in what constitutes a 'fact' for Hosea and for us is a basic requisite. Within Hosea's perspective, there is no difference between the 'event' of Yahweh finding Israel in the desert, Yahweh's 'turning over' of Admah and Zeboim (11.8),[2] the military operations and political machinations alluded to in Hos. 5.10-14, and the destruction of Beth Arbel by Shalman (10.14). Whereas an analysis of the conceptual and programmatic level of historiography may help to relegate the 'nonevents' from the real world to the world of human thoughts and ideas, historical knowledge provides a context

---

belongs to the original text of Judg. 5.5, his geographical context is constituted by 'Edom' and 'Sëir', areas that hardly qualify as 'deserts' ('Sëir' = 'woodland', 'Edom' = 'land of red soil'). I personally prefer a Midianite homeland for Yahweh, but want to stress that the Midianite culture of the expiring Bronze Age was a culture of peasants on the periphery of Canaan and not what one would usually conceive of as a 'desert culture'.

1.   The widespread attitude of Old Testament scholars to credit every pre-exilic Israelite with traditions, knowledge and beliefs that became the traditions, the common knowledge and the beliefs of the postexilic community by accepting as 'canonical' a literature that was created by a small minority of religious and political men (I am sorry, but female authors do not seem to be involved after the archaic period characterized by Exod. 15.21 and Judg. 5) reflects an even more widespread misapprehension of 'folk literature'. In all cases that have been investigated, 'folk literature' is a phenomenon of literary reception, not production. Cf. B. Lang, *Monotheism and the Prophetic Minority. An Essay in Biblical History and Sociology* (SBWAS, 1; Sheffield: Almond Press, 1983); W. Rösler, *Dichter und Gruppe. Eine Untersuchung zu den Bedingungen und zur historischen Funktion früher griechischer Lyrik am Beispiel Alkaios* (Munich: Fink, 1980), pp. 26-114; E. Hobsbawm and T. Ranger (eds.), *The Invention of Tradition* (Cambridge: Cambridge University Press, 1983).

2.   It is not clear whether Hosea refers to a historical event (as in 10.14) or to a mythical 'event' (thus Deut. 29.22). What is clear, however, is that such a distinction would have been irrelevant for Hosea.

within which Hosea's comments on the war of 734 BCE become a meaningful source, which in turn contributes details to the events of that war.[1] In order not to argue in circles, it is essential that the features that anchor some of Hosea's prophecies to 734 BCE not be identical with the features added to the repertoire of 'historical events' from Hosea's prophecy. Where outside control, which in this case is provided by Isaiah, Micah, geography, and the inscriptions of Tiglath-pileser III, is lacking, the historian and the exegete are in no better position than are the epigraphers who frequently read letters that were not meant to be read by them and which presuppose important contextual information that was known by the sender and receiver, but is unknown by their modern (and, according to international postal rules, quite illegitimate) readers.

We always need external evidence, but sometimes there is none. Then, historical criticism still has the function of clearly stating what we do not and cannot know, which at least turns our ignorance into educated ignorance and allows us to state more precisely what we do not know. Shalman and Beth Arbel provide a primary example of this function of circumscribing ignorance (Hos. 10.14). Although we can make a reasonable guess about where Beth Arbel was, based on toponymy and a consideration of the location and relative prominence of the sites that may have preserved the name, we are at a loss as far as Shalman's identity and his destruction of the town are concerned.[2] In this case, archaeology is not helpful at all. Always deficient when it comes to the level of events (admittedly, the earthquake by which the prophecy of Amos is dated appears in the archaeology record at Succoth/Tell Deir 'Alla and other sites),[3] archaeology proves espe-

---

1. Cf. A. Alt, 'Hosea 5, 8–6, 6. Ein Krieg und seine Folgen in prophetischer Beleuchtung', *NKZ* 30 (1919), pp. 537-68 (reprinted in *Kleine Schriften zur Geschichte des Volkes Israel*, II [Munich: Beck, 1953], pp. 163-87); H. Donner, *Israel unter den Völkern. Die Stellung der klassischen Prophetie des 8. Jahrhunderts v. Chr. zur Aussenpolitik der Könige von Israel und Juda* (VTSup, 11; Leiden: Brill, 1964), pp. 42-63; J.M. Asurmendi, *La Guerra Siro-Efraimita: Historia y Profetas* (Valencia: Institución San Jerónimo, 1982).

2. Cf. C.J. Lenzen and E.A. Knauf, 'Chronique archéologique: Irbid (Jordanie)', *RB* 95 (1988), pp. 239-47; C.J. Lenzen, 'Tell Irbid and its Context: A Problem in Archaeological Interpretation', *BN* 42 (1988), pp. 27-35. S. Timm (*Moab*, pp. 318-20) cautions against any attempt to identify Shalman.

3. Cf. Amos 1.1 and H. Weippert, *Palästina in vorhellenistischer Zeit*, p. 626.

cially frustrating in the case of Hos. 10.14 and Beth Arbel, as everything post 800 BCE seems to be bulldozed on top of Tell Irbid.

Hosea and the Structures of his World

It is on the level of structures and processes that historical criticism displays its full potential. There can be no doubt that Hosea interpreted the Assyrian threat that resulted in the final destruction of the Israelite state as Yahweh's punishment for Israel's religious deviation (7.16; 8.4-10; 9.1-3; 10.3, 7-8, 15; 14.1). This attitude implies the opinion that, if Israel would have believed in the right god in the right way, the state would have survived. Here, the modern historian cannot help but contradict the prophet: the growth of empire—*the* empire— from the 9th century BCE through the 2nd century CE was a long-term process effected by a growing Mediterranean world economy that increased the Mediterranean world' wealth, power and interconnection (especially in the case of those who were in control of it).[1] Israel (or any other population group in the mountainous hinterland of the Levantine coast) could not affect or alter this process by anything that it did or believed. One way or the other, the country had no choice but to become, sooner or later, a part of the Assyrian (and finally the Roman) empire. People may have had a choice of politics as far as the details of incorporation were concerned—peaceful integration or self-destructive violence. People always have choices (as have historians), even though they may not always be aware of them. With his concept of cosmological repercussions for Israel's actions, Hosea was hardly aware of the viable political options that his namesake, the king, had between 734 and 724 BCE. This particular blindness does not seem to be restricted to ancient history and ancient Near Eastern societies.[2]

From a purely humanitarian point of view, the last king of Israel made the worst of all possible choices when he rebelled against a lost cause. His belief in the power of Yahweh to turn the course of the

---

1. For the process of the economic and political unification of the ancient world, see A.B. Knapp, *The History and Culture of Ancient Western Asia and Egypt* (Chicago: Dorsey, 1988); Knauf, 'Migration of the Script'; *idem*, 'King Solomon's Copper Supply'.

2. Cf. B.W. Tuchman, *The March of Folly. From Troy to Vietnam* (London: Sphere Books, 1985), pp. 2-40; *idem*, 'Afterward', in *The Guns of August* (New York: Bantam Books, 1976), pp. 484-89; *idem*, *The Distant Mirror* (New York: A.A. Knopf, 1978), esp. chs. 6, 21, 25, 26.

world might have been similar to Hosea's belief; nor was it for the first or the last time that a firm religious or political conviction resulted in catastrophe and slaughter. The unimpeded march of folly toward doom seems to form one of the few indisputable constants of history. On the other hand, the destruction of Israel apparently proved its critic Hosea right and guaranteed the preservation of his intellectual heritage. Israel might have adopted another policy in 724 BCE and so might have avoided terrible human suffering. Then, however, there probably would not be a book of Hosea, nor a Hebrew Bible.[1]

Hosea apparently was proven right, but we have to add, for the wrong reasons. Being virtually proven right, his program of the right service of the right god survived, although initially only transmitted as a minority position.[2] By 588 BCE (and at various occasions later), his concept of history began to shape history.

Although the level of structure and process is not explicitly recognized in biblical historiography, we would be wrong if we assumed that ancient Israelites were not aware of it. Hosea's literary pupil and successor Jeremiah seems at least to have been aware of the unavoidable integration into the empire when he decreed Nebuchadnezzar to be Yahweh's servant, *'ebed* (27.6). In Jeremiah's view, Israel is no longer the world (as it was for Hosea); now, Israel has become a small part of a very large world. Concomitantly, he seems to be the first

---

1. If the Mosaic Creed needs a founder, one could nominate Hosea. His reshaping of religion according to the paradigm of love introduced an element of fervor, personality and intensity into the relationship between humanity and its gods that was to make history. Of course, Hosea would have rejected any such title: for him, all truth was to be found in a mythical past. In general, the founders of religions are constructs of the religious communities that claim their inheritance. It is perfectly possible to reconstruct a hypothetical historical Moses, Jesus or Mohammed. It is not possible to construct empirical theories about God or the gods. Therefore, no god spoke to the historical Moses or resurrected the historical Jesus, and no angel appeared to the historical Mohammed. It is the privilege of faith to be aware of another reality that does not square with our common sense construct of 'the real world'.

2. Cf. B. Lang, *Prophetic Minority*. The evidence compiled by J.H. Tigay (*You Shall Have No Other Gods. Israelite Religion in the Light of Hebrew Inscriptions* [HSS, 31; Atlanta: Scholars Press, 1986]) may be interpreted to reflect the penetration of Judah's ruling class by Hoseanic concepts in the course of the 7th century BCE. His evidence is insufficient for 'monotheism' outside this class and prior to that period.

biblical author who conceived of the world as being one and of Yahweh, its creator and its universal lord, as being well beyond the ethnic limits of Israel.[1] Israel and Israelites are advised to accommodate to a continued existence within that larger world and outside of Israel's land (29.1-23). Jeremiah was a pupil of Hosea, although a very innovative one. His persecutors and tormentors, the leading politicians in Judah between 622 and 586 BCE, were also followers of Hosea. Their intellectual heritage is transmitted through the work of their sons and grandsons that commonly is known as the 'deuteronomistic history'.[2] Reminding their community in 598, if not earlier, of Hosea's evaluation of Israel's conduct in 724 BCE, they knew that this time Yahweh was on their side. Jeremiah did not agree. As we know only too well, he remained a voice in the wilderness with his political insight, and in 586 BCE history repeated itself.

The deuteronomistic history is an attempt to incorporate the experience of 586 BCE and Jeremiah's criticism of the last Judean kings into what is basically a Hoseanic concept: Yahweh produces history in response to Israel's acts. Ancient histories, like their modern counterparts, are theoretical constructs that incorporate empirical data.[3]

1.   Jeremiah's Yahweh, as a universal god, remains the individual's god well beyond the demise of that person's state and nation (Jeremiah 45)—something that the national deity of Israel and Judah, Yahweh, son of El, never could have achieved. Jeremiah dared to think of a great god in a large world. His conservative contemporaries could not follow him. I am aware of the obstacles raised against the construction of a historical Jeremiah by R.P. Carroll (*Jeremiah* [Old Testament Guides; Sheffield: JSOT Press, 1989]), but I agree with N. Lohfink ('Die Gattung der "Historischen Kurzgeschichte" in den letzten Jahren von Juda und in der Zeit des babylonischen Exils', *ZAW* 90 [1978], pp. 319-47) on the intimate relationship between the authors of 6th-century biblical literature and their heroes.

2.   Cf. R. Albertz, 'Die Intentionen und die Träger des Deuteronomistischen Geschichtswerks', in *Schöpfung und Befreiung. Für Claus Westermann zum 80. Geburtstag* (ed. R. Albertz *et al.*; Stuttgart: Calwer Verlag, 1989), pp. 37-53 and previously Lohfink, 'Die Gattung der historischen Kurzgeschichte'.

3.   Ancient history is as much a construct as modern history, sometimes even using similar constructional devices. There remain, however, irreconcilable differences concerning the intelligibility of the world and the dignity of the earthlings. Cf. H. Cancik, *Grundzüge der hethitischen und altestamentlichen Geschichtsschreibung* (ADPV; Wiesbaden: Otto Harrassowitz, 1976); Knauf, *Ismael*, pp. 96-99; H. Weippert, 'Geschichte und Geschichten. Verheissung und Erfüllung im deuteronomistischen Geschichtswerk', in Pentateuchal and Deuteronomistic Studies

However, they are closed systems that allow for the criticism of persons acting in history, but not for the criticism of the system's theoretical presuppositions. For Jeremiah, it was a painful experience to realize how far Yahweh and his acts are beyond human grasp and understanding (forcefully put forward in his 'confessions', and in ch. 45, the conclusion of the first edition of his prophecies).[1] For the deuteronomists and their successors, failure in history still could be avoided by serving the right god in the right way with no further discussions. They believed in a predictable god, the purveyor of a predictable future—an early example of what Popper aptly christened 'the misery of historicism'. Accordingly, in 70 CE history repeated itself once more.

No Conclusion

Historical criticism exhibits biblical history as a thoroughly human history after all, maybe as a paradigmatic human history. The study of history, including biblical history, is not for those who look for corroborations of their claims, justification of their programs, and 'proof' of their theories. Too much damage, intellectually, politically and personally has been and still is done in such a pursuit of a bad dream. The study of history calls for the open-minded who regard dialogue to be higher than declarations of unchallengeable belief and questions higher than answers; who prefer going their own way over remaining with, or arriving at, the crowd. Preferring the road rather than the destination means to accept one of the basic structures of human existence: for mortals, there are no more than preliminary destinations to reach and preliminary results to achieve. Our final destination reaches us.[2]

After talking so much about paradigms and constructs, theories and data, I cannot help reminding myself that after all, I am not just deal-

(BETL 94; ed. C. Brekelmans & J. Lust; Leuven: Leuven University Press, 1990).

1. Cf. H. Weippert, 'Schöpfung und Heil in Jer 45', in *Schöpfung und Befreiung. Für Claus Westermann zum 80. Geburtstag* (ed. R. Albertz *et al.*; Stuttgart: Calwer Verlag, 1989), pp. 92-103.

2. The insight that not possession of knowledge, but the desire to acquire and improve knowledge constitutes humanity's humanity can be traced from Qoheleth through St Paul, St Augustine, William of Ockham, G.E. Lessing and I. Kant to K.R. Popper.

ing with an array of numbers and figures on a white sheet of paper. Behind these numbers and figures, there once were quite real bodies of flesh and blood who are no more. It is easy to formulate theories about the ancients: they cannot sue us for libel. The least that we, the undeservedly fortunate survivors of too many wars (declared and undeclared, past and present) can do for those who no longer share with us the light of the sun is never to forget what our figures imply. It is impossible not to write history in the interest of those presently living, but it should be possible to write it in a way that does not defile the dignity of the dead.

As a German, I cannot think about history, cannot even think about the word 'history' and the concept of history, without thinking of my nation's guilt and shame. The German contribution to the history of the 20th century necessarily tints my outlook on history in general: it foils attempts to derive glory, justification and pride from history (except for the dignity and pride inalienably endowed in every human being). Of course, in an age of multiple identities, there is more than one history that is my history. There is also the history of the Judeo-Christian god who created women and men to be free, who repeatedly led them out of bondage, and who repeatedly resurrected when states (or societies) tried to entomb him in the graven image of the ruling ideology's supreme being. There is also the European history of thinking freedom that originated in the Greek *polis*[1] and will lead beyond Popper. All in all, however, history appears to me more as a history of failure rather than of success, human suffering rather than human achievements, folly rather than wisdom. People are seldom aware of what they are doing when making history, but they make it all by themselves; there is nobody else to blame. The theologian may still add a word on grace and redemption, but this is definitely the point where the historian has to quit (since it is not in the power of the living to grant or demand reconciliation with the dead). What the historian can offer is a final word on history: we do not only have to know history in order to deal reasonably and responsibly with ancient texts, we are also morally obliged to know history in order to finally stop history from repeating itself.

1.   Cf. K. Raaflaub, *Die Entdeckung der Freiheit. Zur historischen Semantik und Gesellschaftsgeschichte eines politischen Grundbegriffs der Griechen* (Munich: Beck, 1985).

TEXT, CONTEXT AND REFERENT IN
ISRAELITE HISTORIOGRAPHY[1]

Thomas L. Thompson

The dictum of Wellhausen that a biblical document reflects the historical context of its own formation rather than the social milieu of its
explicit referents to a more distant past[2] is one that has hardly been
overcome by any of the attempts to synthesize traditio-historical and
archaeological research during the past century. The Altean and
Albrightean syntheses of biblical and extrabiblical research,[3] especially when viewed in the light of the encyclopedic accomplishments
of a Galling or a de Vaux,[4] have only intensified the Wellhausean
impasse. From another direction, the analysis of the prehistory of the
Pentateuch's documentary traditions, following the leads of Gunkel,
Eissfeldt, Noth and Nielsen,[5] has substantially modified perceptions of

1. Diana Edelman is to be thanked for many substantial improvements in the
style and content of this paper. However, faithfulness to its context in the discussion
at Anaheim prevents me from making any extensive revisions.
2. J. Wellhausen, *Prolegomena zur Geschichte Israels* (Berlin: de Gruyter,
1905), p. 316. This dictum played a central role in the development of his
evolutionary history of Israelite religion.
3. Cf. A. Alt, *Kleine Schriften* (3 vols.; Munich: Beck, 1953); W.F. Albright,
From the Stone Age to Christianity (Baltimore: Johns Hopkins University Press,
1940; 3rd edn, 1957).
4. Cf. K. Galling, *Biblisches Reallexikon* (Tübingen: Mohr, 1977); R. de
Vaux, *L'histoire d'Israel* (2 vols.; Paris: Gabalda, 1971).
5. Cf. H. Gunkel, *Das Märchen im alten Testament* (Tübingen: Mohr, 1921);
idem, *Genesis* (ATD; Göttingen: Vandenhoeck & Ruprecht, 1966); O. Eissfeldt,
Einleitung in das alte Testament (Tübingen: Mohr, 1965); *idem*, 'Stammessage und
Novelle in den Geschichten von Jakob, und von seinen Söhnen', in *Eucharisterion,
Gunkel Festschrift*, I (Göttingen: Vandenhoeck & Ruprecht, 1923), pp. 56-77;
M. Noth, *Überlieferungsgeschichte des Pentateuchs* (Stuttgart: Kohlhammer, 1948);
idem, *Überlieferungsgeschichtliche Studien*, I (Königsberg: Niemeyer, 1943);

the historical contexts of traditions and redactions. Such analysis has lent support particularly to the now axiomatic assumption, strongly influenced by the 'biblical theology' movement, that the traditions originated in events.

These post-Wellhausean scholarly movements have shared a common goal and common presuppositions. The goal was to reconstruct the history of Israel's past and of its origins through a historical-critical appraisal of the complex biblical tradition. It was commonly assumed that the tradition's literary fixation first came about during the time of the United Monarchy or slightly later. The existence of a considerable oral prehistory of the texts that leads back to the central core of the tradition's referents in a yet more distant past was taken for granted. This assumption that the traditions maintained an 'essential historicity', or that they were 'rooted' in historical events of the past, is fundamental to an understanding of a historical period of the Judges, and, for some, of even more distant 'Mosaic' or 'patriarchal periods'.

In spite of these substantial changes, the essential thrust of Wellhausen's axiom continues to haunt us, illustrating a perspective necessary to an understanding of the biblical traditions through their historical context. As archaeologically oriented historical scholarship has finally adjusted its assumption that biblical and extrabiblical research are open to direct synthesis, mutual confirmation and conjectural harmonization, much progress in the secular history of Palestine for the Bronze and Iron Ages has become possible.[1] Moreover, as traditio-historical assumptions of a historical core to biblical traditions have been questioned and gradually abandoned, this direction of research has found value and legitimacy as an aspect of compositional theory.[2] It has also become a viable method for one significant aspect of Israel's history; for the development of the tradition reflects the historically significant formative process by which 'Israel', through its use of tradition, was created out of the political and historical disasters

E. Nielsen, *Oral Tradition* (London: SCM Press, 1954).

1. Cf. H. Weippert, *Palästina in vorhellenistischer Zeit* (Munich: Beck, 1988); G.W. Ahlström, *A History of Ancient Palestine* (Sheffield: JSOT Press, forthcoming).

2. T.L. Thompson, *The Origin Tradition of Ancient Israel*, I (JSOTSup, 55; Sheffield: JSOT Press, 1987); idem, *The Early History of the Israelite People* (Leiden: Brill, forthcoming).

of the Assyrian and neo-Babylonian periods. The formation of biblical narrative—this ideologically motivated, originating process that makes Israel—begins at the earliest during the course of Assyria's domination of Palestine. At the latest, the Israel we know from the tradition comes to be during the pre-Hellenistic postexilic period.[1] In the twilight and destructions of the states of Samaria and Jerusalem, the Israel of tradition first presents itself to history, like the phoenix, ever in the form of an *Israel redivivus*, whose true essence and significance—and future glory—is traced in the legends of the patriarchs, of the wilderness and the Judges, and of the golden age of the United Monarchy. Idealistic sentiments of futuristic incipient messianism ring throughout this revisionist tradition with the recurrent affirmation of one people and one God. It is this God, the only true king and emperor, who will some day, finally, really rule from his throne in the temple of the future Jerusalem and who will draw all nations to him through his chosen remnant. This is the Israel of tradition.

To understand the orientation of this literature to any real world of history, renewed focus needs to be given to the context and referent of the text. This is Burke Long's challenge: Does this sacred book render history?[2] I have often argued that it does not. Nevertheless, I agree with Axel Knauf's recent objection to the tendency of my 1987 volume *Origin Tradition* to deny that the literary figure of Abraham 'betray(s) any historical traits'. In fact it does; or perhaps more accurately, at least it must. How it does is not yet clear. Yet Knauf is most certainly correct: the text cannot be divorced from its historical context without loss or grave distortion. Certainly, the near-generational hemorrhaging of literary critics from any serious effort at historical criticism is a huge disaster, diminishing biblical studies through growing ignorance of the world from which our text comes.

Knauf points to a strong tendency, to a categorical error, and reasserts the obvious for all of us who are inclined to the easy road of ahistorical exegesis: even totally 'fictional heroes... reflect the time,

---

1. See also on this E.A. Knauf, 'The Archaeology of Literature, and the Reality of Fictitious Heroes', *Scandinavian Journal for the Old Testament* 6 (forthcoming); *idem, Midian: Untersuchungen zur Geschichte Palästinas und Nordarabiens am Ende des 2. Jahrtausends* (ADPV; Wiesbaden: Otto Harrassowitz, 1988).

2. B.O. Long, 'On Finding the Hidden Premises', *JSOT* 39 (1987), pp. 10-14.

place, and conceptual world of their authors'. This is axiomatic for any serious study of literature from the past. No text is understood apart from its context. However difficult historical criticism may be and however uncertain its conclusions, the questions it asks are adamantly fundamental to reading and have no alternative. Only a text that we ourselves write, and even that for only a brief fleeting time, can be read univocally and simplistically as a coherent, signifying, holistic entity created fully—whole and entire—in itself in its final form. And this is so, not because we are aware of the process of its formation and may be ignorant of that process in the work of another, but rather, more sacramentally, because we, as authors, in its final form, signify it as such. It is that final form that we own and not its sources, nor its many drafts.

If a text, however, presents itself to us as a composite, a holistic and univocal reading of its final form significantly distorts that text unless we can reasonably believe that the final form was a significant and inherently functional construct of that given text's composition and not a unity and reality given to it externally. Such an external unity and reality could arise, for example, through its inclusion centuries after its composition in an extraneous, and to its world foreign, canon. We must always ask about those structural unities of a text that signify meaning. All meaning-bearing structures, to the extent that they are translatable, have a historical contingency or context that must be unlocked if we are to make it ours. Meaning does not signify apart from a historical context, real or assumed. Historical-critical thought is nothing more than the systematic task of reducing the blindness and ignorance of our assumptions.

The final form of most biblical texts rarely purports to be a unit whole in itself. Within a canon, biblical texts never do. Anthological, historiographic and archival motives and functions are so common that the signification of much of what the extant form brings together bears meaning primarily in marked independence from the context in which it is collected and only secondarily as an element of a larger context. I submit that this distinctive peculiarity of so many of the units of biblical tradition is the result of their having been collected as meaningful traditions in themselves. They are voices apart from the collector, historiographer, or archivist, that spoke to them, as they do to us, from the past.

An insistence on analysis from the perspective of the final form of the tradition is valid insofar as what is meant is that our point of departure is the extant biblical texts. This is valid because it requires us to read the texts we have and not some other more imaginary traditions. This is an issue of authenticity and the directness of our observation of evidence; it is the issue of objectivity.

However, what is at times spoken of as a canonical reading of biblical tradition is essentially misleading to anyone who wishes to discover the signification of the tradition that was Israel's. Such reading distorts the tradition from the perspective of a theologically biased ideological orthodoxy of late antiquity. Such canonical context has no relevance either to the biblical tradition's original signification, nor does it bear any intrinsic meaning of the text for us. The value added to these texts by their canonical context is extraneous and intrinsically separate from them. The wishful thinking of this socalled criticism may have its place in formulating theological *desiderata*. Canonical criticism certainly has an important role to play in early church history—but it does not belong in a field that purports to speak critically about ancient Israel and about the literature of that ancient people,[1] who had neither a canon nor anything that can be described as a 'biblical community'.

The assumption that the process of the formation of the canon was already an aspect in the process of Torah composition[2] not only takes far too much for granted in Pentateuchal composition theory, but anachronistically projects a social construct such as a rabbinate back into the early Persian period. Even an assumption of such a social reality

1. The understanding of Brevard Childs (*Introduction to the Old Testament as Scripture* [London: SCM Press, 1979]) that canon began already in the early Israelite period is certainly anachronistic, as is The assumption of James Sanders (*Torah and Canon* [Philadelphia: Fortress Press, 1972]) about a 'biblical community' in the early and pre-Persian periods. T. Sheppard's presentations (*Wisdom as a Hermeneutical Construct: A Study in the Sapientializing of the Old Testament* [Berlin: de Gruyter, 1980], and esp. *idem*, 'Canonization: Hearing the Voice of the Same God through Historically Dissimilar Traditions', *Int* 36 [1982], pp. 21-33) are substantially more sophisticated. N.K. Gottwald's incisive criticism of Childs's tendencies to dehistoricize theology and the reading of scripture ('Social Matrix and Canonical Shape', *Theology Today* 42 [1985], p. 320) cannot be overstressed. However, his attempts to trace an analogy to the 'canonical process' in a legendary revolutionary tribal confederation (p. 313) totally lacks historical warrant.

2. As presented by S.Z. Leiman, *The Canonization of Hebrew Scripture: The Talmudic and Midrashic Evidence* (Hamden: Ktav, 1976).

dominating the early Palestinian Judaism of R. Akiba (110-135 CE) stretches credulity unnaturally. The coercive essence of canonicity reflects a historical contingency that goes well beyond mere literary context or favored lists of divinely favored manuscripts. It is normative in character and, as such, necessitates a norm-producing and sustaining context, a situation that did not pertain either in Judaism or Christianity before the 4th-6th century CE. It is hardly before the late 1st and 2nd centuries CE that competing lists and the validity of the now Christian LXX for Judaism might be seen to focus attention on the limits of the sacred. A more likely period—subsequent to the unanimity of so-called canonical lists—for canonical coerciveness of Akiba-like intensity would be the doctrinal and gnostic controversies of the following 3rd to 5th centuries in which both Judaism and Christianity first began to form their distinctive orthodoxies. It is in this context of incipient orthodoxy that origin legends about Yavneh such as those of Yohanan ben Zakkai and Vespasian[1] and, on the Christian side, about the LXX such as the 'Letter of Aristeas' helped establish the foundations of a new conservative traditionalism. Similarly, perspectives such as 'audience-response' criticism have a tremendously important historical-critical role to play, not only in regard to Knauf's essential historical context of narrations and their successive revisions, but also throughout subsequent stages in the text's history of interpretation, where audience and eventually canonical context became two foci of one continuing project of interpretation.

An example might be useful. To understand the LXX as translation is a thoroughly profitable orientation when a scholar is attempting to reconstruct the various possibilities of Hebrew *Vorlage* that may have existed in the 2nd-1st centuries BCE. Such a perspective would provide an invaluable and necessary historical context for questions asked of the text. Similarly, to read the LXX as literature requires the assumption—and hopefully the explication—of the historical context of that text in the 2nd century BCE. However, to read the LXX as Luke–Acts' Bible requires an understanding of an entirely different historical context, the explication of which involves such issues as the similarities of Luke's Bible to extant manuscripts of the LXX, as well as an

---

1. Cf. J. Neusner, 'Beyond Historicism after Structuralism: Story as History in Ancient Judaism', *Henoch* 3 (1981), pp. 171-99, esp. pp. 189, 194-95.

investigation of the enormous differences that exist between Hellenistic Alexandria and the Greco-Roman world of the New Testament.

To confuse such thoroughly historical-critical subgenres of both tradition and church history with the reading of a literature that is understood as directly relevant to today's audience (i.e. the Bible of Judaism and Christianity) is to make a historically contingent blunder. That is religion, not biblical scholarship. Such a blunder is comparable to the anachronistic metaphysics of many sociological approaches to Israel's history.

It is wholly unacceptable to assume even for a moment that the text, metaphysically transcending historical context, is not of a very specific past. The past context of a text must always form a part of any contemporary understanding. It was written in a now dead language within a culture that ceased to exist more than two millennia ago. Although a substantial core of Israelite tradition has survived until today in the form of our much later extant manuscripts, any perspective, theological or literary, that starts from the mythical premise that biblical texts exist in themselves or speak directly to us, having us for their audience, is more uncritical than simply ahistorical.[1] That some of these efforts, such as 'structuralism', claim to seek an objectivity in their research compounds our problems. What is 'objective' is the extant text that exists apart from any contemporary reader. Old texts hold images, meanings and intentions that are as historically contingent as the images, meanings, and intentions of very specific individuals now long dead. To discover their signification is the task of exegesis. The neofundamentalistic rejections of historical criticism I have mentioned, while bypassing its problems, leave little hope of understanding texts of the sort we find in the Bible. The primary point of departure for critical exegesis is and always remains historical con-

---

1.   Such a perspective is to be expected in theologically oriented exegesis and may even be understood as legitimate in the context of homiletics. I have rather in mind such efforts as those of R. Alter (*The Art of Biblical Narrative* [New York: Basic Books, 1983]) on one hand, and of D. Jobling (*The Sense of Biblical Narrative* [JSOTSup, 7; Sheffield: JSOT Press, 1978]) on the other. An interesting discussion of some of these issues is found in R.N. Whybray, 'On Robert Alter's, *The Art of Biblical Narrative*', *JSOT* 27 (1983), pp. 75-86, esp. pp. 77-78, and in D. Jobling, 'Robert Alter's, *The Art of Biblical Narrative*', *JSOT* 27 (1983), pp. 87-99.

text, which enables us to recreate the conceptual world of the tradition's authors.[1]

The specific manner in which we find this historical context and conceptual world refracted by the tradition requires yet further discussion. Unfortunately, Pentateuchal scholarship, and traditio-historical literary criticism generally, are not yet at the point at which we can reconstruct history directly from tradition. The interpretive problem involving the historical changes that moved the people of ancient Palestine to forge a sense of ethnicity out of the political and military disasters that overtook the indigenous states of Samaria and Jerusalem at the hands of the Assyrians and Babylonians is one that can hardly be dealt with apart from an understanding of the initial formulation and development of the specific traditions and ideologies that first gave expression to this ethnicity. These traditions and ideologically motivated perspectives are not so much direct refractions of ancient Israel's past as they are themselves intrinsically and substantially causative forces in the development of what, in spite of our dependence on these perceptions, we today understand as Israel.[2] As Max Miller has clearly and convincingly argued, any examination of the origins of Israel is forced to move in lock step with an examination of the development of Israelite tradition.[3] Apart from biblical tradition, this Israel never existed as a historical reality open to independent historical research and judgment. It was in the formation of the tradition as such that—to borrow a phrase from Malamat—Israel of tradition, for the first time, became a dominant reality in the history of ancient Palestine.[4] From this perspective, one must agree with Miller's conviction that Israel's tradition is in a radical and fundamental way our starting point for the history of Israel.[5] Without it,

1. Similarly, Neusner, 'Beyond Historicism', p. 196.
2. This does not involve a judgment about the historicity of many aspects of the biblical tradition, especially of 2 Kings, but addresses only the process by which older narratives and historiographical sources are understood as traditions about an Israel, which, transcending its pre-exilic status as the state of Samaria, takes on the contours of the Israel of tradition (cf. also G. Garbini, *History and Ideology in Ancient Israel* [trans. J. Bowden; New York: Crossroad, 1988]).
3. Orally at the annual convention, SBL, Chicago, 1988.
4. A. Malamat, 'Die Frühgeschichte Israels: eine methodologische Studie', *TZ* 39 (1983), pp. 1-16.
5. J.M. Miller and J.H. Hayes, *A History of Ancient Israel and Judah*

we cannot write a history of Israel, because, within the context of the Persian renaissance, the tradition itself created the population of Palestine as Israel out of the ashes of the Assyrian and Babylonian empires.

Biblical tradition is related to Israelite history when we use it teleologically and understand Israel as the end result of a literary trajectory. If, however, we use the tradition as historical evidence for a history prior to the historical context of the tradition, such a history can hardly avoid being anachronistic in its essence. Nevertheless, when understood teleologically, the tradition gives focus and direction to our research; for it is the Israel of tradition that we need to explain historically.

I hope it is true that the great divide between Genesis 11 and 12, demarcating myth from history or heroic epic, has finally disappeared from our textbooks. Nowhere in the narrative tradition of Genesis–2 Kings do we have such a watershed.[1] The stories within this extended tradition generally bear the character of 'traditional narratives' that stand somewhat apart from both history and historiography.[2] Chronicles, Ezra and Nehemiah also do not stand substantially closer to a recoverable 'history', for they too took their shape long after the events of which they might be thought to speak. The purported referents of these later works are also distinct from their contexts. Nor is the intent underlying their collection so obviously a historiographic one, however much they have been structured chronologically.[3] Any

(Philadelphia: Westminster Press, 1986).

1. *Contra* J.A. Soggin, 'The Davidic and Solomonic Kingdom', in *Israelite and Judaean History* (ed. J.H. Hayes and J.M. Miller; Philadelphia: Westminster Press, 1977), p. 332. Cf. my 'History and Tradition: A Response to J.B. Geyer', *JSOT* 15 (1980), pp. 57-61, esp. pp. 59-60. See also J. Rogerson, *Myth in Old Testament Interpretation* (BZAW, 134; Berlin: de Gruyter, 1974).

2. Following here D. Gunn, *The Stories of King David* (JSOTSup, 4; Sheffield: JSOT Press, 1976).

3. Cf. P. Welten, *Geschichte und Geschichtsdarstellung in den Chronikbüchern* (WMANT, 42; Neukirchen–Vluyn: Neukirchener Verlag, 1973); H.G.M. Williamson, *Israel in the Book of Chronicles* (Cambridge: Cambridge University Press, 1977); R.L. Braun, 'Chronicles, Ezra and Nehemiah: Theology and Literary History', in *Studies in the Historical Books of the Old Testament* (ed. J.A. Emerton; Leiden: Brill, 1979), pp. 52-64.

interpretive matrices, which we may be tempted to draw from the biblical story itself, render for us only hypothetical historical contexts, events, and situations whereby our texts only seem to take on meaning as literary responses. The matrix, however, remains imbedded in the literary vision and is not historical.

This danger of eisegesis is particularly serious when assumptions akin to Eissfeldt's imaginary *Stammesgeschichte* are present,[1] where fictional stories are understood as refracted pantomimes of supposedly real political and social struggles. As with other forms of allegorical interpretation, these efforts bypass all critical evaluation.[2] Fairly mainstream historical-critical exegetical efforts are implicated in this criticism. For example, recent scholarly efforts have tried to associate such a central tradition complex as Numbers 16–18 with a presumed historical Levitical conflict in the pre-exilic period or to an equally imaginary postexilic Aaronide hegemony over the cult.[3] Both options are unverified fictions, created wholly from the traditions themselves. They share the common categorical error of assuming the very history they seek to reconstruct. Similarly, the increasingly common temptation to associate the Abraham wandering tales or the Exodus stories with a historical context in the exile, interpreting these stories as implicit reflections of the return and of the exiles' self-understanding as *gērîm*, is equally suspect.[4]

Not even the Pentateuch's golden calf story or Bezalel's construction of the Ark and tent of meeting can, with any reasonable security, be related to any alleged historical matrices by making them retrojections of presumably reliable depictions of cultic innovations under-

---

1. O. Eissfeldt, 'Stammessage und Menscheitserzählung in der Genesis', in *Sitzungsberichte der Sächsischen Akademie der Wissenschaften zu Leipzig* (Phil-hist K1 110, 4; Berlin: Akademic-Verlag, 1965), pp. 5-21.

2. See my 'Conflict Themes in the Jacob Narratives', *Semeia* 15 (1979), pp. 5-26.

3. Cf. J. Milgrom, 'The Rebellion of Korah, Numbers 16-18: A Study in Tradition History', in *SBL Seminar Papers* (ed. K.H. Richards; Atlanta: Scholars Press, 1988), pp. 570-73 and E. Rivkin, 'The Story of Korah's Rebellion: Key to the Formation of the Pentateuch', *SBL Seminar Papers* (ed. K.H. Richards; Atlanta: Scholars Press, 1988), pp. 574-81.

4. Here I am reacting to my own inclination to reinterpret these traditions as stories *originating* in an exilic or early postexilic context. Cf. my *Origin Tradition*, pp. 194-98.

taken by the Jeroboam and Solomon of 2 Kings. The tales of 2 Kings are also traditions, not history, and as traditions they are fully equivalent to their variants set in yet more hoary antiquity.

One does well to reflect on both the multivalent and distinctive nature of so many of the traditions found within biblical historiography. We find parallel patterning of narration in such tradition variants as the two crossings of the sea in Exodus and the comparable miracle at the Jordan in Joshua, or in the recurrent use of common motifs as in Genesis 16 and 21 or 12, 20, and 26, Genesis 19 and Judges 19, Gen. 12.10 and Ruth 1.1. Equally importantly, however, are the variant traditions of 'events' such as in Genesis 10 and in 11.1-9; or in the accounts of the three distinct conquests of Jerusalem and of Lachish. Similarly, there are variant persons of biblical heroes—not only the many Abrahams, or the two or more Moseses of the prewilderness narratives, but also the two Judahs: the son of Jacob and the first of the Judges. Apart from a consideration of the many lost traditions unavailable to us, the immense complexity involved in the history of the extant traditions alone must give pause to any scholar employing a method of historical research that prefers one element of the tradition as more viable historically than another. Without concrete external evidence, such selective preference is not critical. As long as we continue to work with historical contexts that are not based on independent evidence, plausibility and verisimilitude cannot be recognized as valid criteria for historicity. Plausibility and verisimilitude are characteristics that are to be attributed even more to good fiction. Reasonableness is far more a characteristic of the fictional genres of literature than it is of history. History happens; meaning and coherence are created.

When we are dealing with univocal traditions without extant variants we have precious few[1] means which enable us to recognize and confirm positively a reference to a real past[2] or to measure in any significant way the manner and extent to which the tradition reflects its

1. This lack is rapidly diminishing in recent years, not only through the dozens of monographs and hundreds of articles that have revolutionized the history of Palestine, but also through the recent comprehensive handbooks of Helga Weippert, *Archäologie Palästina* and Gösta Ahlström, *History of Ancient Palestine*.

2. For an earlier discussion of some of these issues, cf. my 'Conflict Themes', pp. 5-26.

own historical context. Valid negative conclusions are many, come immediately to hand, and certainly do not need emphasis in this forum.[1] Knauf's suggestions for the analysis of the various discrete social contexts in our tales certainly carry us in the right direction. However, our need to situate such potentially relevant contexts geographically and chronologically is, given the known variability and constant flux in human societal forms, all the greater if the suggestions and the methods involved are ever to be trusted.

Moreover, the recognition and clarification of explicit and implicit referents and conceptual contexts do not define the limits of the positive contributions to be expected from a study of the historical world of our narratives. Of equal importance is the growing realization that the redactional techniques of the comprehensive traditions of the Pentateuch, of the so-called deuteronomistic tradition and of their variants in Chronicles–Ezra–Nehemiah reflect not merely the occasional historiographical intentions of the redactors, but also and more frequently the pedantic, antiquarian efforts of curiosity and preservation.[2] These are not only distinct from historiography but at times inimical to it. Historians ask the question of historicity and critically distinguish and evaluate their sources. They 'understand' history and therefore often slip into tendentious ideologies and theologies—so Thucydides.[3] The antiquarian, on the other hand, shares the more

1.   One might note the discussions in M. Weippert, *Die Landnahme der israelitischen Stämme in Palästina* (Göttingen: Vandenhoeck & Ruprecht, 1967); T.L. Thompson, *The Historicity of the Patriarchal Narratives* (BZAW, 133; Berlin: de Gruyter, 1974); J.H. Hayes and J.M. Miller (eds.), *Israelite and Judaean History* (Philadelphia: Westminster Press, 1977); J.A. Soggin, *The History of Israel* (Philadelphia: Westminster Press, 1984); N.P. Lemche, *Early Israel* (VTSup, 37; Leiden: Brill, 1985); Miller and Hayes, *A History of Israel and Judah*; Garbini, *History and Ideology*.

2.   Recent comparisons of biblical narrative with Greek authors, especially Herodotus (cf. J. Van Seters, *In Search of History* [New Haven: Yale University Press, 1983] and R.N. Whybray, *The Making of the Pentateuch* [JSOTSup, 54; Sheffield: JSOT Press, 1987]), underscore the importance of this more detached scholarly aspect of our traditions. *Pace* Van Seters, such detachment is to be contrasted to the more politically and ideologically motivated genre of historiography. Cf. further on this, my article 'Historiography' in the forthcoming *Anchor Bible Dictionary*.

3.   The issue here is not one of historicity but of historiography and pertains to the intention of the author, not his success. On this, see the interesting discussion of

ecumenically pluralistic motivations of the librarian (not without significant discrimination and occasional critical control) classifying, associating, and arranging a cultural heritage that is greater than both the compiler and any single historiographical explanation—so perhaps Herodotus,[1] Philo of Byblos,[2] and certainly the Pentateuch![3]

W.R. Connor, 'Narrative Discourse in Thucydides', in *The Greek Historians: Literature and History*, A.E. Raubitschek Festschrift (ed. W.R. Connor; Saratoga: Saratoga University Press, 1985), pp. 1-17; P. Robinson, 'Why Do We Believe Thucydides? A Comment on W.R. Connor's "Narrative Discourse in Thucydides"', in *Greek Historians*, pp. 19-23; and S.W. Hirsch, '1001 Iranian Nights: History and Fiction in Xenophon's Cyropaedia', in *Greek Historians*, pp. 65-86.

1. For recent discussions of historiography in Herodotus, cf. H.R. Immerwahr, *Form and Thought in Herodotus* (Philological Monographs, 23; Cleveland: Western Reserve University Press, 1966); H. Fahr, *Herodot und altes Testament* (EHST 23, 266; Frankfurt: Lang, 1985); P.R. Helm, 'Herodotus' Medikos Logos and Median History', *Iran* 19 (1981), pp. 85-90; K.D. Bratt, 'Herodotus' Oriental Monarchs and Their Counsellors' (dissertation, Princeton University, 1985); J.M. Balcer, *Herodotus and Bisitun* (Historia, 49; Stuttgart: Steiner, 1987); H. Sancisi-Weerdenburg, 'Decadence in the Empire or Decadence in the Sources?', in *Achaemenid History*, I (ed. H. Sancisi-Weerdenburg; Leiden: Brill, 1987), pp. 33-45; F. Hartog, *The Mirror of* Herodotus: *The Representation of the Other in the Writing of History* (trans. J. Lloyd; The New Historicism: Studies in Cultural Poetics, 5; Berkeley: University of California Press, 1988).

2. Cf. H.W. Attridge and R.A. Oden, *Philo of Byblos: The Phoenician History* (CBQMS, 9; Washington DC: Catholic Biblical Association, 1981). Other ancient Near Eastern historiographic ethnographies and related genres might profitably be compared with Old Testament literature and themes. Cf., e.g., W.W. Hallo, 'Assyrian Historiography Revisited', *Eretz Israel* 14 (1978), pp. 1*-7*; *idem*, 'Sumerian Historiography', in *History, Historiography, and Interpretation* (ed. H. Tadmor and M. Weinfeld; Leiden: Brill, 1984), pp. 9-20; *idem*, 'Biblical History in its Near Eastern Setting: A Contextual Approach', in *Scripture in Context* (ed. W.W. Hallo, C.D. Evans and J.B. White; Pittsburgh: Pickwick Press, 1980), pp. 1-26; N.E. Andersen, 'Genesis 14 in its Near Eastern Context', in *Scripture in Context*, pp. 59-78; P. Veyne, *Did the Greeks Believe in Their Myths?* (Chicago: Chicago University Press, 1988); F. Rochberg-Halton, 'Fate and Divination in Mesopotamia', *Archiv fur Orientforschung* 19 (1982), pp. 363-71; M. Liverani, 'The Ideology of the Assyrian Empire', in *Power and Propaganda*, (ed. M.T. Larsen; Mesopotamia, 7; Copenhagen: Academisk 1979), pp. 297-317; P. Michalowski, *The Lamentation over the Destruction of Sumer and Ur* (Winona Lake, IN: Eisenbrauns, 1989); M. Weinfeld, 'Divine Intervention in War in Ancient Israel and in the Ancient Near East', in *History, Historiography and Interpretation*, pp. 121-47; H. Tadmor, 'Autobiographical Apology in the Royal Assyrian

The recent discussions by Giovanni Garbini, Axel Knauf, and especially by David Jamieson-Drake[1] of the ancient scribal profession, issues involved in book formation and library collections have all agreed that we cannot seek an origin of literature in Palestine prior to the 8th, or perhaps even better, the 7th century BCE at the height of Judah's influence in the hill country north of Jerusalem that had formerly been part of the state of Samaria. An 8th or 7th century historical context pertains not only to the conceptual world of the narrators of biblical tradition, but equally as powerfully to the world of the collectors of those narrations.[2]

Literature', in *History, Historiography and Interpretation*, pp. 36-57; H. Cancik, *Mythische und Historische Wahrheit* (SBS, 48; Stuttgart: Katholische Bibelwerk, 1970); *idem, Grundzüge der Hethitischen und alttestamentlichen Geschichtsschreibung* (ADPV; Wiesbaden: Otto Harrassowitz, 1976).

3.   Cf. Van Seters, *In Search of History*; Whybray, *Making of the Pentateuch*; Thompson, *Origin Tradition*. For a dissenting voice on the comparison between the Pentateuch and Herodotus, cf. R.E. Friedman, 'The Prophet and the Historian: The Acquisition of Historical Information from Literary Sources', in *The Past and the Historian* (HSS, 26; ed. R.E. Friedman; Cambridge, MA: Harvard University Press, 1983), pp. 1-12. Some important recent studies of Israelite historiography are: H. Schulte, *Die Entstehung der Geschichtsschreibung im alten Israel* (BZAW, 128; Berlin: de Gruyter, 1972); M. Weippert, 'Fragen des israelitischen Geschichtshewusstseins', *VT* 23 (1973), pp. 415-41; G.W. Trompf, 'Notions of Historical Recurrence in Classical Hebrew Historiography', in *Studies in the Historical Books of the Old Testament* (VTSup, 30; ed. J.A. Emerton; Leiden: Brill, 1979), pp. 213-29; D.I. Block, 'The Foundations of National Identity: A Study in Ancient Northwest Semitic Perceptions' (dissertation, University of Liverpool, 1981); R. Schmitt, *Abschied der Heilsgeschichte?* (EHST, 195; Frankfurt: Lang, 1982); J.A. Soggin, 'Le Origini D'Israele Problema per lo Storiografo?' in *Le Origini di Israele* (Rome: Accademia nazionale dei lincei, 1987), pp. 5-14; B. Halpern, *The First Historians* (New York: Harper & Row, 1988); Garbini, *History and Ideology*.

1.   Garbini, *History and Ideology*; Knauf, *Midian*; and D. Jamieson-Drake, *Scribes and Schools in Monarchic Judah: A Socio-Archaeological Approach* (SWBAS, 9; Sheffield; Almond Press, 1991). Cf. further on this the earlier related studies of Rogerson, *Myth in Old Testament Interpretation*; A. Lemaire, *Les écoles et la formation de la Bible dans l'ancien Israel* (OBO, 39; Göttingen: Vandenhoeck & Ruprecht, 1981); and Halpern, *First Historians*.

2.   That the Old Testament is a 'collection' or even a library of literature, authored by many different persons, is a commonplace of biblical studies. The perception, however, that this description also accurately describes the *function* of the collection of traditions of Genesis–Ezra–Nehemiah as library, substantially explaining the textual context of the works included in this collection, was first

In a world that knows libraries, not only does the nonutilitarian function of writing find room to expand and proliferate, but the genre of the collected literature itself undergoes structural alteration. Tales are linked and become chains of narration, which in turn, can extend in a theoretically infinite succession of chains. In the broad conceptual context of a library, chronology, the linear progression of a series of heroic persons or the great periods and epochs of the past steps outside of the semantic and historiographic nuances of past, present and future and provides an order and structure that is uniquely external to the literature itself. Chronology becomes capable of relating a multiplicity of literature within a comprehensive framework. The resulting succession of episodes and narratives has only the appearance of history.

The collection of literature from Genesis–2 Kings was expanded in the late Persian or early Hellenistic period with Chronicles, Ezra, and Nehemiah and even later with the Megilloth. Many of the extended traditions contained in this library have survived because they were 'popular' or because they were 'in demand'; that is, they found echo and meaning in the lives of their possessors, the handful of collectors and those limited few who used books for leisure. For them, these traditions held relevance for both their political and social worlds, often lending these fragmented worlds of experience interpretive contexts of their own. One ought not to assume, however, that such *Sitze im Leben* lie *im Leben des Volkes*. Rather, we are dealing only with a small handful of scholarly bibliophiles.[1]

We cannot then assume that the traditions as such necessarily reflect either indirectly or explicitly the real world of their tradents and collectors. They are only meaningful to that world either in terms of contemporary signification or of a more distant future projection. The issue of the sources for the final compositions and collections is of critical importance in understanding our text. It is in the context of the discrete traditions themselves being from the past that we come to

granted me by the observations of S.E. Janke in a seminar in Jerusalem in 1985. That there is not a normative role in such collections or anything at all similar to a canon is obvious.

1. These, however, do not form a class of 'elite'. Uncritical assumptions such as B. Lang's (*Monotheism and the Prophetic Minority* [SWBAS, 1; Sheffield: Almond Press, 1983]) seeming equation of literacy and political and economic dominance is without historical justification—anywhere or anytime.

deal for the first time with the originating signification of their historical context. Our understanding of collectors and redactors, such as the author of the *tôlᵉdôt* structures of Genesis or the collector of the wilderness variants found in the second half of Exodus and in Numbers does not supply us with that primary context which can be understood as a historical matrix of tradition. Nor can the world of such compilers be understood as the referent of the tradition, that is, the situations or events which the tradition is about. Rather, research into the historical context of such redactions, even of a 'final' redaction, renders only a secondary usage and perspective, only a world in which our traditions have become meaningful or useful. This world was earlier than, but nonetheless comparable to, the much later *Sitz im Leben* of the traditions in one or another canon of the early church or synagogue.

From the perspective of the world of the collectors, we do not understand the historical referent. Nor are we able to reconstruct specific historical and sociopolitical contexts that somehow (with Knauf) must be reflected in such traditions from the past, whether or not they have been fragmented and transformed by these secondary contexts. In addition, the more the narrator or collector of such composite traditions is convinced that the 'realities' of such traditions represent the distant past or more recent events, or are significant to his world-view, the less we will be able to understand his sources in their own context and signification. To the extent, on the other hand, that they have not been transformed by their inclusion in this 'library' and by their association with the other discrete works that surround them—each with its own context, referent and intention—to that extent they become amenable to a historical-critical analysis of both their originating context and their historicity. In addition, the traditions become open to being understood in their own terms, meanings and intentions, apart from what they have been made to mean in the accumulating, distinct contexts of their tradents.

The issues of whether or not the biblical traditions of Genesis–2 Kings and Chronicles–Ezra–Nehemiah are literarily unified, dealing with Israel's past *ex novo*, whether they are primarily tendentious, ideological and/or theological historiographic redactions of traditions, whether they are oral or literary, or whether they are the gatherings of a bibliophile or librarian are of immense interpretive importance. That they are traditions of the past is the primary *raison d'être* for their inclusion. How past they are is a subject of examination for each recognizably distinct tradition collected.

The nature of both the manner of composition and the tendentiousness of historiography, however, renders it exceedingly difficult to recognize and distinguish the discrete sources of historiography. What we can know is largely restricted to the understanding of the world and of tradition at the time of the writing of the historiography. Even when a more ancient source is claimed by the putative historian, our judgment regarding the veracity of such claims must derive almost totally from the world we understand to be contemporary with the historiography. The pursuit of a specific *Traditionsgeschichte* must by necessity be limited to the analysis of changes that are specifically observable in the text, and even such observable transitions may reflect a variety of contemporary understandings rather than an evolutionary development that might carry us into a prehistory of the text. The unproven assumption that the Pentateuch tradition is historiographical and the creation of a single literary hand—perhaps undergoing successive revisions and editions by subsequent authors[1]— can speak only to the successive secondary contexts within which the growing tradition finds a home. In only a limited fashion does it speak to our tradition's originating matrices or significant referents. Such historiographic traditions must be seen as largely irrelevant to critical historical reconstruction because any questions regarding the sources or bases of the successive author's assumptions and perspectives are essentially closed to us. Also lacking is any criterion for establishing either a relative or absolute chronology for strata within the tradition. Indeed, we lack criteria for confirming the existence of any distinctive strata at all, since the basis for the recognition of distinctive ideologies is itself derived primarily from internal considerations without any demonstrable relationship to any realities apart from the text, which at least *prima facie*, is a unit. To assume that J^2, for example, is to be dated to the exilic period because it is easier to interpret it within that context is wholly inconsequent as a historical-critical evaluation. However much the process of this tradition formation might presumably reflect the worlds of the redactors or collectors, each with their

---

1. I am thinking here for instance of such as the revisionist hypothesis of Van Seters (*Abraham in History and Tradition* [New Haven: Yale University Press, 1975]).

distinctive political, social and religious realities, it can hardly be used directly for reconstructing these worlds that are largely unknown to us. Even less can they be used for a reconstruction of the circumstances and events of the tradition's past referent. The tradition, within its field of semantic references, lives within both a real and a literary world. Without a detailed and independent understanding of the historical contexts within which a tradition has relevance, our ability to distinguish or even identify the historical contexts of the tradition is fleeting and sporadic. Furthermore, both the historiographic and antiquarian concerns that sought to preserve traditions after the collapse of the old order do not pretend to present any coherent or univocal truth about the past.[1] Unlike the collections of laws at Qumran, but comparable perhaps to the seemingly omnivorous collections of tradition found in Greek literature or those attributed to Yavneh, the efforts at tradition collection and preservation reflected in the Pentateuchal and deuteronomistic corpora grew out of the collapse and destruction of the societies of Samaria and Jerusalem. It was these disasters that gave the traditions and tradition fragments a historical context as collection and meaning as revered tradition.

However, the specific content of the narratives that have been suspended out of their own time and held as meaningful to these late pre-exilic, exilic, and postexilic tradents does not directly reflect either the exilic or the postexilic world in which the traditions have found their final form. The narratives do not even reflect the pre-exilic world they so desperately tried to preserve. Like the traditions of Yavneh, the biblical traditions reflect only incoherent, part-fictive remnants of a past that the survivors of the destruction and their descendants were able to put together and give meaning to in the radically new worlds into which they were thrown.

It is their significance as meaningful expressions of the old order, giving hope and direction to the new that affected these traditions' preservation, not their dependability in preserving past realities, so painful and ineffective as they were. Both the form and the content of the preserved past have been strongly affected—I hesitate to use the

---

1.   One might note an analogous indifference to a thoroughgoing ideology in the efforts made to collect the traditions of the schools of Hillel and Shammai by Hillelites after the fall of Jerusalem in AD 70. Cf. J. Neusner, *From Politics to Piety* (New York: Orbis, 1979), p. 100.

word determined—by the needs of the tradents. Understandably, the realities of the referents were often perceived as having less significance.

It is indisputable that many elements of the received tradition reflect the exigencies of the exilic and early postexilic periods. Yet other elements refer to what has become a fictionalized or literary past. Clear examples of a past existing in literature only are the referents of the immensely instructive phrases in Exod. 15.26d and 23.21. The appeal to 'Yahweh, your healer', in 15.26d is out of context in the tale episode of 15.22-26, wherein Yahweh neither plays nor is called upon to play the role of healer. Nor does this divine title derive from the larger context of Exodus 1–23, where Yahweh provides and protects, guides and saves, but never heals. On the other hand, the close variant tradition found in Num. 21.4-9 presents a deity with whom the motif of healing might be associated, and another variant in Deut. 7.12-15 not only presents Yahweh as healer, but also refers to a now lost account of an episode in Egypt in which Israel, too, suffered disease. It is noteworthy that Yahweh's healing is presented as a reward for obedience to his ordinances in both Exod. 15.22-24 and Deut. 7.12-15. A process of literary allusion, not historical reference, is apparent here.

Even more striking is Yahweh's speech to Moses in Exodus 23. In its context of the early constitutional tradition of Exodus 1–24.8, the speech by Yahweh who is sending his angel to lead Moses and his people against his enemies in 'the place [he] has prepared' refers to a future transgression, which Yahweh will not forgive (v. 21). The immediate and original context (23.1–24.8) makes it very clear that the unforgivable transgression to which this speech directs us is Israel's entering into covenants with the peoples and gods of *Eretz Israel*. The referent then is historiographical and external to the tradition. The threatened punishment for this unforgivable transgression refers to the destruction of either Jerusalem or Samaria, understood theologically and ideologically as having been caused by their own God as a result of what is here attested as Israel's fault. The suggested historical context of this original narration is obviously then the post-destruction period, either the 7th or the 6th centuries. This context is perhaps *pre*-Persian since the potential transgression is understood as unforgivable. Yet this must remain uncertain as the remnant ideology of postexilic prophetic tradition epitomizes Yahweh's mercy with the forgiveness of the unforgivable.

Within the context of the whole of the Pentateuch our pericope of Exod. 23.20–24.8 radically alters its referent. No longer does Yahweh's speech reflect immediate preparations for the conquest of Palestine. Rather, it serves as an opening to the wilderness wandering. The book of the covenant that Moses wrote (Exod. 24.4, 7) is quickly displaced by Yahweh's tablets (Exod. 24.12), themselves displaced by Moses' copy (Exod. 34.4-6, 27-29) as he runs up and down the mountain for successive variations on the traditions of Exodus 19 and 20. Within this context, the referent is literary and internal. It is the transgression of continued murmuring and the sins of Miriam and Aaron, and of Aaron and Moses, in the growing conglomerate of narrative, explaining the entrance into the Promised Land of a new generation rather than the generation addressed by Yahweh in Exodus 23. The historical context of this literary referent is apparently the postexilic situation in which the tradition supports the hope of a new generation in Palestine who have identified with the return from the 'wilderness' of exile to the Promised Land. This hope is born, or promises to find its fulfillment, in their lives in the Persian period.

Although many primary elements of the tradition reflect the historical contexts of periods earlier than the received tradition's formation, their narrative contexts, both primary and secondary, imply a historical context associated with the complex secondary level of the tradition. This suggests in turn that the compilation of the extant tradition is, in terms of intellectual history, clearly distinct from its sources. Such a distinction between an originating historical context (i.e. historical matrix) and a secondary historical context is particularly pertinent when dealing with traditions that appear to be largely irrelevant to their received contexts, yet assumed by this secondary context to derive from hoary antiquity. Here one might well think of Leviticus 16, but perhaps also those tales introduced into larger narratives by means of 'postintroductory inclusion'[1] such as Gen. 12.10-20, Genesis 26 and Genesis 38. It is equally necessary for the historical critic to sort out the potentially distinctive literary and historical referents and contexts of narratives that appear to exhibit

---

1.   Cf. Thompson, *Origin Tradition*, p. 169.

historiographical or literary harmony (e.g. Gen. 11.26–12.4)[1] or an editorial dovetailing of successive variant narrations of what was perceived as an equivocal episode or tale (e.g. Gen. 6–9; Exod. 5–13; and Exod. 14).[2]

Given the complex manner in which the tradition has functioned as survival literature, our ability to relate the historical context of various redactive moments to the late pre-exilic, the exilic, or the postexilic periods does not substantially help our arriving at either the specific historical and intellectual milieu of their received form or, ultimately, the specific sociohistorical matrix of their origins, except in the grossest and most general terms. As survival literature, the traditions render a composite ideological understanding to these periods. The traditions are not so much a direct reflection of or reference to their periods of origin and composition as they are an explanation that gives meaning to them. That is, the ideological and theological *Tendenz* of the received or extant traditions, to the degree that they are oriented to the world of the final stages of the tradition's formation, may well preclude their use for any historical reconstruction based on assumed events from a greater past. For such past worlds refracted from the redactions are constructs of a world contemporary to the redaction. Indeed, they stand outside of any historical field of reference other than intellectual history. The historical significance of the received tradition, holistically perceived, lies primarily in its dual functions as meaningful literature and as library in post-compositional times.

One must indeed incline towards the Persian period for the historical context in which our narratives have their significance as a tradition of Israel. At such a late date considerable portions of the tradition's original contextual content have already lost much of their intrinsic relevance. While these traditions have been transvalued in the process of transmission and have acquired an even wider meaning than they bore as reflections of the often opaque world of their original historical context, they have also lost much cohesion with their specific origins in antiquity.

Unlike the problems surrounding the historical context of a literary unit, the problem dealing with their intentional referent involves one

---

1. Thompson, *Historicity of the Patriarchal Narratives*, pp. 308-11.
2. Cf. Thompson, *Origin Tradition*, pp. 74-77, 139-46.

immediately with the many variant degrees of fictional and historiographical intent as well as with the externally oriented issues of
accuracy and historicity. Internally, one necessarily distinguishes
a number of discrete formal categories as relevant: (a) aetiologies,
(b) traditional tales, (c) *Standesgeschichte*, (d) *Stammesgeschichte*,
(e) genealogical tales, (f) romances, (g) ethnographies, and (h) his-
toriographies.[1] Their intentional referent distinguishes them. For
instance, aetiology is different from historiography in that the referent of an aetiology is typically some contemporary reality, while
historiography refers to the perceived past. Historiographical narrative is distinct from the often literarily comparable traditional tale in
that historiography involves a critical reflection on sources for the
past with the intention of presenting the reality of the past, while
traditional narratives are preserved either for antiquarian motives
(because they are from the past) or because of their hermeneutical and
heuristic value to the tradent. Propaganda, on the other hand, and
other ideologically tendentious literature are essentially anticritical,
intending to distort or to create a past for extraneous reasons.
Stammesgeschichte, Standesgeschichte, and genealogical tales, with
their signification born of attraction to the tradents, are all essentially
subvarieties of historiography, propaganda or romances. Romances
are distinct from traditional tales in that they are fictional histories
and literary expressions of the aura surrounding the heroes and events
of the past. Certainly Genesis 14 fits this category (*pacem* Cancik!),
perhaps the song of Deborah in Judges 5, and with little doubt the
song in Exodus 15.

Only very few Israelite narratives involve historiography at a primary level of the tradition.[2] This genre is most notably present in the
larger redactions and final forms of composition. Even there, a comprehensive, historiographically motivated critical perspective rarely
surfaces in our literature. The sweeping assertions common today that
boldly refer to 'historians' and the like existing long before

1.   Cf. further my article 'Conflict Themes', pp. 5-26.
2.   On this particular issue, see the early chapters of either Miller and Hayes,
History of Israel and Judah or Soggin, *History of Israel*. The more recent and more
radical presentations of N.P. Lemche (*Ancient Israel: A New History of Israelite
Society* [Sheffield: JSOT Press, 1988]) and Garbini (*History and Ideology*), though
less comprehensive, are closer to the writer's position; cf. my *Early History of the
Israelite People* (forthcoming).

Thucydides[1] say much more than they properly can.

The hard times that have come upon historical-critical research in its effort to write a history of Israel reflect a positive growth in awareness of the biblical tradition's lack of historicity and historiography. Much of the historical-critical research of the past that has been written in reaction against Wellhausen has been committed to the preservation of these two endangered species and has supported the now defunct dogma that a critical history of Israel is rendered through a synthesis of biblical archaeology and biblical criticism.

Very recent efforts to write a history of the United Monarchy as a development from the sedentarization of the central hill country in terms of Saulide and Davidic 'chieftainships' are to be commended for many reasons. They attempt a new synthesis of archaeological evidence and biblical tradition, while at the same time dealing competently and critically with the issues of historiography and historicity.[2]

1. I am thinking here of such otherwise helpful studies as Van Seters's *In Search of History*. One might also refer to similar assumptions of B. Long ('Historical Narrative and the Fictionalizing Imagination', *VT* 35 [1985], pp. 405-16) and C. Meyers ('The Israelite Empire: In Defense of King Solomon', in *Backgrounds for the Bible* [ed. M.P. O'Connor and D.N. Freedman; Winona Lake, IN: Eisenbrauns, 1987], pp. 181-97). See, on the other hand, the very interesting discussion of H.M. Barstad ('On the History and Archaeology of Judah during the Exilic Period: A Reminder', *Orientalia Louvaniensa Periodica* 19 [1988], pp. 25-36).

2. Most notable among these studies are: Lemche, *Ancient Israel* and I. Finkelstein, *The Archaeology of the Israelite Settlement* (Jerusalem: Israel Exploration Society, 1988). The Chicago dissertation of D. Edelman ('The Rise of the Israelite State under Saul' [1986]; see also especially her 'Saul's Rescue of Jabesh Gilead [1 Sam 11:1-11]: Sorting Story from History', *ZAW* 96 [1984], pp. 195-209; and her 1989 paper, 'The Deuteronomist's Story of King Saul: Narrative Art or Editorial Product?', in *Pentateuchal and Deuteronomistic Studies* [BETL, 94; ed. C. Brekelmans and J. Lust; Leuven: Leuven University Press, 1990], pp. 207-20) deserves particular focus both because of its critical control of much of the recent progress in Palestinian archaeology, but also because of its detailed concentration on the tales of the 'United Monarchy' that are historically the most viable. Because of this heuristic value, the following remarks have Edelman's dissertation most in mind. The recent 'holistic' interpretation of the David stories by J. Flanagan (*David's Social Drama: A Hologram of Israel's Early Iron Age* [SWBAS, 7 and JSOTSup, 73; Sheffield: Almond Press, 1989]) on the other hand, does not share Edelman's control of the archaeological material and takes a largely uncritical perspective of the biblical tradition. Consequently, it is of less value for a

The hypothesis of the existence of 'chieftainships' in the central hills of Palestine during the Iron I period, identified as the historical reality from which the biblical traditions sprang, is useful for illustrating the benefits and pitfalls of synthetic reconstructions of the history of Palestine. This is particularly true of the hypothesis of a 'Saulide chieftainship'. Not only are some, perhaps primary episodes of the biblical narrative isolated, but the historical reality of such a political structure, limited to the central hills of Palestine as J.M. Miller has long argued,[1] can be justified as possible with considerable persuasiveness.[2] The arguments for such a synthesis, however, must, given the lack of specificity in our archaeological sources, proceed along the lines of verisimilitude—what is often perceived as 'probability'. The strength of such a model, based as it is on historical-like observations of a Finkelstein-like archaeological summary of surveys and excavations in the hill country,[3] is considerable as long as a close association between Iron I Ephraim and the Israel of tradition can be maintained. The validity of such a comprehensive hypothesis, however, does not directly relate to these issues, even when the archaeologically oriented discussion appears most persuasive. The validity of any such synthetic hypothesis, even when carried out with detail and care, stands or falls on issues of historiography and historicity. Some of the difficulties of accepting a Saulide chieftainship as a historically viable reality, in spite of the truly impressive archaeological illustration of such hypotheses are as follows.

1. Given the more recent datings of 1–2 Samuel, there exists a three-to-four-century gap between the biblical tradition and the reconstructed events to which the 'primary' traditions supposedly refer. This weakness is particularly awkward since the necessary continuity between a hypothetical Saulide chieftainship and the royal dynasties of the state of Samaria, and through them with the Israel of tradition, is essentially supported by an obviously fictional, or at least fictionalized

theoretical and methodological discussion.

1. J.M. Miller, 'The Israelite Occupation of Canaan', in *Israelite and Judaean History*, esp. pp. 213-45.

2. Edelman, 'Rise of the Israelite State', who, however, argues for a Saulide kingship, not a chieftainship.

3. Finkelstein, *Archaeology*.

association with the legendary Davidic dynasty of a neighboring state.[1]

2. Secondly, following the line of argument developed in Israeli scholarship by B. Mazar, Y. Aharoni and M. Kochavi, there is an assumed equation of the sedentarization of the central hills of Iron I with the origins of the state, which is later known in both tradition and international politics as Israel.[2] In spite of objections to a simplistic identification of the pre-Saulide Iron I settlements as 'Israelite', this equation allows an association of the Saulide chieftainship with the Iron I settlements of this region, in spite of the lack of historical warrant for that identification.

3. This caution is intensified by the observation that we are also lacking any direct evidence for a process of regional centralization in the central hills before the foundation of Samaria during Iron II. Thus, such an association in the Iron I period remains in the realm of mere possibility.

4. To assert the existence of a historico-political entity 'Israel' as early as Iron I—however small a 'chieftainship' or 'kingship' that might be—seems to create enormous difficulties for illustrating political continuity and unity: continuity with the state of Samaria in Iron II and unity with the early settlements of other regions, including the Jezreel Upper Galilee and the Iron II sedentarization of Judah. To relate, for exam-

1. I am thinking here, for example, of the well-worn numerical motif of 40 for the number of kings between Saul and the Judean exile.

2. Cf. esp. B. Mazar, *Canaan and Israel* (Jerusalem: Mošad Bialik, 1974); *idem*, 'The Early Israelite Settlement in the Hill Country', *BASOR* 241 (1981), pp. 75-87; Y. Aharoni, *The Settlement of the Israelite Tribes in Upper Galilee* (dissertation, Jerusalem, 1957); *idem*, 'New Aspects of the Israelite Occupation in the North', in *Near Eastern Archaeology in the Twentieth Century, Glueck Festschrift* (ed. J.A. Sanders; New York: Doubleday, 1970), pp. 254-65; *idem*, 'Nothing Early and Nothing Late: Rewriting Israel's Conquest', *BA* 39 (1976), pp. 55-67; M. Kochavi, 'The Period of Israelite Settlement', in *The History of Eretz Israel. II. Israel and Judah in the Biblical Period* (ed. I. Eph'al; Jerusalem: Israel Exploration Society, 1984), pp. 19-84; *idem*, 'The Land of Israel in the 13th-12th Centuries B.C.E. Historical Conclusions from Archaeological Data', in *Eleventh Archaeological Conference in Israel* (Jerusalem: Israel Exploration Society, 1985), p. 16; Finkelstein, *Archaeology*. In his paper at the 1990 SBL Convention in New Orleans Finkelstein rejected the necessity of this association.

ple, a hypothetical Davidic chieftainship with the Hebron and
northern Negev region does not lighten the problem of
continuity, however judiciously these associations might be
expressed and however much it may help bypass issues of
historicity with arguments of comprehensiveness bolstered by
plausibility.

5.   The greatest problem of such synthetic reconstruction
touches upon the paramount issue of the effervescent relationship between biblical literature and historical research.
One cannot but question any alleged 'reliable pool of information'. Reminiscent of the syntheses of the Albright school
in the fifties and sixties, the concept of a Saulide or Davidic
state or chieftainship is a hybrid, bearing little resemblance
to either the Israel of tradition or the historical associations
potentially derived from archaeology. Real historical issues
are not those infinite ones of possibility and necessity (history
is *Wissenschaft*, not metaphysics), but rather those of reconstruction, related to evidence established. If historicity cannot
be granted to the biblical tradition as a whole or even to very
specifically defined parts of it, why should we be tempted to
adopt a perspective that is derivative from the comprehensive
tradition? Why should we assume that Saul's kingdom was a
precursor to the Davidic monarchy and had its roots in the
divinely rejected northern hills? And if such anachronistic
reconstruction cannot be supported, what benefit is derived
from attributing such political unification to Saul? These
efforts to harmonize archaeological evidence and biblical
tradition reminds me of a poem by Milne:

> Halfway up the stairs
> Isn't up, and isn't down.
> It isn't in the nursery
> It isn't in the town.
> And all sorts of funny thoughts
> Run round my head:
> It isn't really anywhere!
> It's somewhere else instead.[1]

In suggesting that the essential interpretive context of the narrative

1.   A.A. Milne, *When We Were Very Young* (London: Dutton, 1972), p. 83

tradition of Genesis–2 Kings is that period during which the tradition achieved its role as survival literature, a perspective is recommended which is quite different from that usually taken by tradition history. Again as Miller has argued, it is unlikely that we will be able to correlate adequately the earlier strata of the tradition with concrete historical events in Israel's past, or even with any of the episodes of the tradition, as if they were, somehow, memories of a real past. Determining the potential historical referents of the tradition and determining that tradition's relevance to the writing of a history of Israel is theoretically more possible the closer we are to the extant form of the tradition. However, this is true only to the extent that these latest formulations and revisions relate to or are identical with those issues and events informing these ultimate redactions.

The hypothesis that the received traditions once existed in antiquity in substantial form at a time prior to these latest redactions needs reinvestigation. Certainly Wellhausean forms of 'documents' dating from as early as the United Monarchy must now be abandoned—if only because of the tenuous hold on existence the period of the United Monarchy has. Furthermore, much recent scholarship has questioned the existence of such extensive and coherent portions of the received text at such an early period and variously recommends a historical context in the late pre-exilic, exilic, or the early postexilic periods.[1] An early date certainly seems impossible now. However, too specific, late dates appear arbitrary and seem based on circular arguments.

Our understanding of the Josianic reform and of the prophetic and convenantal ideologies that presumably supported it is essentially based on a historicistic and naïve reading of 2 Kings,[2] which is, after

---

1. H. Vorländer, *Die Entstehungszeit des Jehowistischen Geschichtswerkes* (EHST, 23.109; Frankfurt: Lang, 1978); Van Seters, *Abraham in History and Tradition*; idem, *In Search of History*; H.H. Schmid, *Der Sogenannte Jahwist: Beobachtungen und Fragen zur Pentateuchforschung* (Zurich: Theologischer Verlag, 1976); Lemche, *Early Israel*; E. Blum, 'Die Komplexität der Uberlieferung: Zur synchronen und diachronen Analyse von Gen 32:23-33', *DBAT* 15 (1980), pp. 2-55; idem, *Die Komposition der Vätergeschichte* (WMANT, 57; Neukirchen–Vluyn: Neukirchener Verlag, 1984); M. Rose, *Deuteronomist und Jahwist* (ATANT, 67; Zurich: Theologischer Verlag 1981); and F. Kohata, *Jaw hist und Priesterschrift in Exodus 3–14* (BZAW, 166; Berlin: de Gruyter, 1986).

2. Lowell Handy's recent paper to the SBL Midwest regional convention in February 1990 at Madison is a serious effort to redress this perspective ('Assyro-

all, a product of the same spectra of traditions that use 2 Kings for their referential context. Similarly, in dating the prophets—Amos, Hosea, 1 Isaiah–Ezekiel—we too quickly assume that the prophetic traditions had original nuclei deriving from the events and persons alleged by the traditions themselves, which continued to have significance in a postdestruction world. In fact, however, we know historically little of such events or persons.

The external confirmatory evidence we have for these assumptions is both fragmentary and oblique. The very knowledge we have of the exilic and postexilic periods rests on the presupposition that Chronicles, Ezra and Nehemiah can somehow be translated into refractions of historical reality. Yet we know that these traditions were also written and edited as substantial traditions of Israel's past long after the exilic and early postexilic periods. Because of this, the assumption that they can render history is no longer obvious and has to be tested with each unit of tradition.

The synthetic approach to historiography, which has dominated our field at least since Eduard Meyer, must now be abandoned. If we are ever to achieve our exegetical goal of allowing the biblical narrative to be heard and understood within the modern context of our discipline, the first and primary need is to establish, in all the fullness and detail possible, an independent history of early Palestine and Israel that might serve as the historical context from which these narratives speak. Without such an interpretive matrix, we continue to read the biblical tradition in faith—as through a glass darkly.

Babylonian Cult Narratives and Historical Probability for Josiah's Reform').

IS IT POSSIBLE TO WRITE A HISTORY OF ISRAEL WITHOUT RELYING ON THE HEBREW BIBLE?

J. Maxwell Miller

In several publications over the past years, I have explored the complex methodological problems involved when one attempts to interrelate nonwritten evidence (artifacts) with written sources for purposes of historical reconstruction.[1] I have observed, for example, that while nonwritten artifacts provide information about general socioeconomic conditions, settlement patterns, life styles and the like, they are silent regarding specific people and events. If we are to know the names of the people who left the artifacts or any specific details about their history, we must rely on written records. Written records are also limited in the kind of information they provide and often give a biased or one-sided impression of things.

I have observed further that, when historians combine artifactual and written evidence to produce historical scenarios, the written evidence tends to take precedence, and there is always some degree of circular argumentation involved. On the first point, that the written evidence tends to take precedence, I mean that it tends to set the definitions and parameters of the scenario and thus determine the way the artifacts will be interpreted in that context, more so than the other way around. Regarding the inevitable circularity, the best a historian can do is try to hold it to a minimum; and one way to do this is to analyze each type of evidence separately, with the tools and methods appropriate to it, and determine what can be learned from this

---

1. Cf. esp. *The Old Testament and the Historian* (Philadelphia/London: Fortress Press/SPCK, 1976), pp. 40-48; 'Archaeology and the Israelite Conquest of Canaan: Some Methodological Considerations', *PEQ* 109 (1977), pp. 87-93; and 'Old Testament History and Archaeology', *BA* 49 (1987), pp. 51-62.

particular kind of evidence alone, before interweaving it with other kinds of evidence.

Consider for a moment the kinds of evidence available for dealing with the origin and early history of Israel. From the artifactual, non-verbal evidence alone (all the foundation walls, potsherds, and what have you, excavated to this point) one would never even surmise that the people known as Israel appeared on the scene in ancient Palestine. Simply to use the name 'Israel' in association with the Iron Age means to draw on written sources. The written sources pertinent for dealing with ancient Israel fall into two categories: materials of various sorts collected in the Hebrew Bible and certain nonbiblical documents (royal inscriptions, for the most part). Most of the nonbiblical documents may be considered first-hand evidence in that they were written soon after the events which they report. Unfortunately, they provide only occasional references to Israel, and without prompting from the Hebrew Bible these references would not tell us much.

Without prompting from the Hebrew Bible, for example, do you suppose it would occur to historians to read the hieroglyphic name of Merneptah's foe in his so-called Israel Inscription as 'Israel' and to recognize it as the equivalent of the Moabite and Assyrian renditions of the name that do not turn up until 350 years later? I doubt it. And what would they make of these later references? Our hypothetical historians (still working entirely with the inscriptional sources and without prompting from the Hebrew Bible) probably would make the connection between 'Omri king of Israel' mentioned in the Mesha Inscription, 'Jehu *mar Humri*' in three of Shalmaneser's inscriptions, and the references to the 'land of *bit-Humria*' in Tiglath-pileser's records. But would they read 'Ahab of *Sir-'i-la-a-a*' in Shalmaneser's Monolith Inscription as 'Ahab the Israelite' or recognize that Samaria, which also turns up occasionally in other Assyrian contexts, was the capital of 'Omri land' rather than some other place altogether? Probably not. And if they did, the general impression derived would be that Israel was a small kingdom, located somewhere in the vicinity of Damascus or the Phoenician coast, apparently founded by one Omri during the first half of the ninth century and surviving to the latter half of the eighth century. I am confident, moreover, that any efforts to isolate the material culture of ancient Israel would follow the lead of these written sources. Rather than talk about Early Iron Age settlement patterns in the central Palestinian hill country, the search would focus on Iron Age II, on southern Lebanon or perhaps Galilee, and would involve widely divergent views regarding the location of Samaria.

Obviously this is not where things stand now in our research, and it is because we rely heavily on the Hebrew Bible. Not the archaeological evidence, nor the extrabiblical sources, nor a combination of the two, but the Hebrew Bible primarily sets the parameters of the ongoing discussion regarding the origin and early history of Israel. Whether this *should* be the case, whether we *should* rely so heavily on the Hebrew Bible is another question that I will address briefly below. For the moment, I am concerned only to observe that this is what we are doing. Any time historians, archaeologists, sociologists, or whoever speak of Israelite tribes in the central Palestinian hill country at the beginning of Iron Age I, or about the Davidic–Solomonic monarchy, or about two contemporary kingdoms emerging from this early monarchy, they are presupposing information that comes from, and only from, the Hebrew Bible.

Now I would have thought that this is self-evident, but apparently it is not, since several recent papers and monographs make rather a lot of the fact that the Bible is an unreliable source of historical information. They take a condescending attitude toward historians who bother with it and they insist that we can deduce a great deal about the origin and early history of Israel quite apart from it.

Coote and Whitelam's recent book, *The Emergence of Early Israel*[1] is perhaps the best example. Pointing out the inadequacies of histories of Israel that rely on the Hebrew Bible and old-time literary-critical methodologies, they proposed 'an alternative approach...which assigns priority to interpreting archaeological data within a broad interdisciplinary framework' (p. 8). Thereupon, without involving themselves with the biblical materials in any direct way, they set about clarifying the socioeconomic circumstances in Palestine during the early Iron Age, explaining how the Israelite tribes emerged under these circumstances and then describing the process by which the tribes were transformed into a centralized, Davidic state. How do they know that Israel's origins are to be associated with the early Iron Age in the first place, or that the tribes were soon transformed into a cen-

---

1.   R.B. Coote and K.W. Whitelam, *The Emergence of Early Israel in Historical Perspective* (SWBAS, 5; Sheffield: Almond Press, 1987).

tralized Davidic state? They appeal to scholarly consensus: 'The most commonly agreed datum to mark the emergence of Israel is the extension of village and agricultural settlement in the central highland of Palestine from the thirteenth to the eleventh centuries BCE' (pp. 27-28). And this is the pattern throughout; either they assume information that can only have come from the Hebrew Bible, or they appeal to scholarly consensus, which itself rests on the Bible. In short, their study does not bypass the Hebrew Bible, it only bypassess any critical evaluation of it. While remaining aloof from the Bible of literary analysis, they assume the essential historicity of the Bible story as they heard it in Sunday school.

Thomas Thompson, in his *The Origin Tradition of Ancient Israel*,[1] characterized the recent history which I coauthored with John Hayes as 'essentially a theological and apologetic work'[2] because of its heavy involvement with the biblical materials and announced that we are on the threshold of a new era with respect to the study of Israelite history. Theological histories such as ours are about to be replaced with scientifically objective ones that rely instead on revolutionary new archaeological evidence and on epigraphical sources.

> It is. . . the independence of Syro-Palestinian archaeology that now makes it possible for the first time to begin to write a history of Israel's origins. Rather than the Bible, it is in the field of Syro-Palestinian archaeology, and the adjunct fields of ancient Near Eastern studies, that we find our primary sources for Israel's earliest history (p. 27).

Presumably Thompson will demonstrate what he has in mind in his next book.

In the meantime William Dever assures us that archaeologists can now isolate the earliest Israelite settlements and tell us a great deal about these earliest Israelites entirely from the material remains. As for my observation that artifacts are silent and remain 'anonymous unless interpreted in the light of written records', he quipped that 'the archaeological data are not mute; but the historian is often deaf'.[3]

---

1.   T.L. Thompson, *The Origin Tradition of Ancient Israel*. I. *The Literary Formation of Genesis and Exodus 1-23* (JSOTSup, 55; Sheffield: JSOT Press, 1987), p. 26.

2.   *A History of Ancient Israel and Judah* (Philadelphia/London: Westminster Press/SCM Press, 1986).

3.   W.G. Dever, 'Unresolved Issues: Toward a Synthesis of Textual and

Dever, of course, like Coote, Whitelam, and presumably Thompson, is associating the Israelites with the early Iron I hill-country settlements. How does he know that these are Israelite settlements? Is there anything about the potsherds or wall lines that cries out 'Israelite'? Certainly not. Dever also is relying on the current scholarly consensus, which itself rests on clues from the Hebrew Bible that have been interpreted to suggest that Israelite tribes must have been settling in that area at about that time. The artifacts are still silent unless interpreted in the light of written documents. And the interpreting document in this case is the Bible.

When claiming that a revolutionary new kind of archaeological evidence is available now for tracing the roots of Israel, our colleagues apparently have in mind the sort of research pioneered by Israel Finkelstein and set forth in his recent book *The Archaeology of the Israelite Settlement.*[1] All of them emphasize the value of comprehensive regional surveys (as opposed to the earlier archaeological work that tended to focus on the stratigraphy of major 'tells'), and all of them are vague on what exactly they mean by 'Israelite'. How, for example, are we to distinguish an Israelite village from a Hivite, Gibeonite, or Kenizzite village? In the final analysis, they beg the question by using 'Israelite' as an all inclusive term for anyone living in a hill-country village during Iron I. According to Finkelstein,

> even a person who may have considered himself a Hivite, Gibeonite, Kenizzite, etc., in the 12th century, but whose descendants in the same village a few generations later thought of themselves as Israelite will, in like manner, also be considered here as an Israelite (p. 28).

Finkelstein proceeds then to describe the material culture of the Iron I villages and trace their spread—which, given his question-begging definition, is the same as tracing the spread of the early Israelite tribes. Tracing the spread requires distinguishing early Iron I sites from later Iron I sites. He mentions several criteria for this purpose, but the only really tangible ones involve the so-called Ark Narrative in 1 Samuel 4–6 and 2 Samuel 6. This narrative describes a

Archaeological Reconstructions?' (Presented in a SBL-ASOR jointly sponsored symposium on the topic 'New Perspectives on the Emergence of Israel in Canaan' at the 1987 annual meeting in Boston).

1.   I. Finkelstein, *The Archaeology of the Israelite Settlement* (Jerusalem: Israel Exploration Society, 1988).

Philistine victory over Israel in the vicinity of Aphek and Ebenezer, and Finkelstein's program requires (a) that the story be accepted as historical; (b) that the battle be dated to the mid-11th century BCE; (c) that Aphek be identified with present-day Ras el-'Ain; (d) that Aphek/ Ras el-'Ain be seen as a Philistine frontier city; (e) that nearby 'Izbet Ṣarṭah be seen, accordingly, as an Israelite village (possibly Ebenezer); and (f) that as a follow up to their victory at Aphek the Philistines overran the central hill country, destroyed Shiloh, and perhaps also Ai and Khirbet Raddana. Assuming all of this, 'Izbet Ṣarṭah III and Shiloh become type-sites for recognizing early Iron I villages (i.e. pre-mid-11th century/pre-battle of Aphek), while the existence of Philistine pottery in a hill-country site marks it as a later Iron I village (post-battle of Aphek).

What if there is a fallacy somewhere in Finkelstein's chain of assumptions? Suppose, for example (just for the sake of argument, if nothing else), that virtually all of the critical commentators who have worked with the Ark Narrative are correct in warning that it is a tendentious literary piece that plays very loose with history at best.[1] Suppose that my interpretation of the narrative is correct, which I have elaborated elsewhere; namely, that this story represents a duplicate account and distorted memory of the Aphek battle that occurred near Mount Gilboa at the end of Saul's reign.[2] This would undercut the Aphek/Ras el-'Ain equation (which is uncertain in any case, as

---

1. Cf. esp. L. Rost, *Die Überlieferung von der Thronnachfolge Davids*, (BWANT, 3; Stuttgart: Kohlhammer, 1926) = L. Rost, *Das kleine Credo und anderer Studien zum Alten Testament* (Heidelberg: Quelle und Meyer, 1856), pp. 119-253; A.F. Campbell, *The Ark Narrative* (SBLDS, 16; Missoula, MT: Scholars Press, 1975); P.D. Miller and J.J.M. Roberts, *The Hand of the Lord: A Reassessment of the 'Ark Narrative'* (Johns Hopkins Near Eastern Studies; Baltimore, MD: Johns Hopkins University Press, 1977); and P.K. McCarter, Jr, *I Samuel* (AB, 8; Garden City, NY; Doubleday, 1980), pp. 23-26. Even Miller and Roberts, who dated the narrative prior to David's victories over the Philistines, recognized that 'it is a thoroughly theological narrative at its very core' (p. 60). 'The whole narrative was not created immediately after the return of the ark. One must assume that the legend grew and developed in response both to doubt and to the storyteller's art, and it was probably affected as well by the growing distance from the historical events' (p. 75).

2. *History of Ancient Israel*, pp. 127, 130; 'Site Locations in the Saul Narratives of I Samuel' (Presented at the southeastern regional meeting of the Society of Biblical Literature, Chattanooga, 1986).

Robert North pointed out years ago[1]), make it very difficult (even with Finkelstein's sweeping definition) to secure 'Izbet Ṣarṭah III as an early-stage Israelite settlement, and lower the date of any village destructions associated with the Aphek battle (Shiloh in particular) from the middle of the 11th to at least the end of the 11th century BCE.

But whether you accept Finkelstein's interpretation of the Ark Narrative or mine, the situation illustrates again my point that when one combines artifactual and written evidence to produce a historical scenario, usually the written evidence takes precedence. It identifies the people who left the artifacts: Finkelstein calls them 'Israelites', not Iron I people. It establishes the historical parameters: these Israelites are understood to have been in the early stages of an expansion and consolidation process, which would result in an Israelite monarchy, which occupied a definable region, which in turn serves to identify the Iron I villages in that region as 'Israelite'. Finally, having established these historical parameters, the written evidence influences significantly the way that the archaeological details are interpreted. Begin with the potsherds, and Khirbet Seilun is an anonymous site with a reasonably impressive building complex that was destroyed sometime during Iron I. Interpreted in the context provided by the Hebrew Bible, it becomes ancient Shiloh, an important Israelite cultic center destroyed by the Philistines in the mid-11th century BCE and thus, a type-site for tracing the earliest stages of Israelite settlement.

Please understand. It is not my intention to belittle the importance of archaeology for historical research. Neither is it my intention (in this presentation) to challenge the assumptions of specific conclusions reached by these colleagues. I also suspect, as a matter of fact, that the early Israelites are to be associated in some way with the early Iron I villages of central Palestine.[2] My purpose rather is to call attention to their indirect (thus uncritical and often muddled) use of the Hebrew Bible and object to their condescending remarks regarding historians who attempt to work with the biblical materials more directly and critically. In my own case, rather than being a biblical apologist, I would say that it is precisely my critical work with the biblical materials that has led me to be more cautious than they regarding its

1. Robert North, 'Ap(h)eq(a) and 'Azeqa', *Bib* 41 (1960), pp. 41-63.
2. *History of Ancient Israel*, p. 85.

historical reliability, apparently more aware than they of the biblically based assumptions that underlie current scholarly consensus, and more hesitant than they to spin out scenarios that involve interweaving Bible and archaeology. More than anything else, I object to the methodological implications of some of their rhetoric.

In the first place, their rhetoric suggests that now, after generations of false starts, we can finally reconstruct with scientific objectivity what really happened in ancient Israel. Theirs, in short, is the talk of positivistic historians. I am more of a relativist, for reasons that I have explained on earlier occasions.[1] When it comes to the origin and early history of Israel, I think the best we can ever hope to do is make some guesses and offer some hypothetical scenarios. These scenarios, moreover, will reveal as much about how we understand our own historical circumstances as what we know about ancient Israel.[2]

Secondly, their rhetoric implies that it is a simple question of deciding whether the Hebrew Bible is a reliable source of historical information and, correspondingly, whether or not to use it in historical research. Of course it is not a reliable source, taken at face value. But neither should it be dismissed as totally irrelevant. Its very existence is a historical fact to be reckoned with. The appropriate question is not *whether* we should use the Hebrew Bible in historical research, but *how* we should use it.

Thirdly, while declaring the Hebrew Bible an unreliable source and depreciating the relevance of literary-critical research for historical investigation, these colleagues ignore the problems and limitations of the other kinds of evidence and the alternative methodologies that they espouse. Having conducted one of the regional archaeological surveys, I must tell you that surveys are not entirely reliable either. The data collected represent a highly selective sampling at best and are usually open to a range of interpretations. As for alternative methodologies, perhaps we need to be reminded that methodologies are ways of examining evidence and never should be mistaken for evidence itself. Coote and Whitelam may have fallen into this trap. Much of their

---

1. 'New Directions in the Study of Israelite History', *Teologiese Tydskrif* 30 (1989), pp. 152-60; 'In Defense of Writing a History of Israel', *JSOT* 39 (1987), pp. 53-57.

2. Cf., e.g., J.M. Sasson, 'On Choosing Models for Recreating Israelite Pre-Monarchic History', *JSOT* 21 (1981), pp. 3-24.

scenario for the origin of Israel, which they advertise as the result of applying new methodology, strikes me as just another hypothesis dressed up in sociological jargon.

Finally, by declaring that archaeology is more reliable than the Hebrew Bible for dealing with the origin and early history of Israel, the rhetoric ignores the extent to which Syro-Palestinian archaeology itself is infused with assumptions derived from the Bible. To put it bluntly, Thompson's remark about the independence of Syro-Palestinian archaeology reflects a misunderstanding of how archaeology works. Regarding ceramic typology, for example, archaeologists can work out a relative chronology from the potsherds alone, but when they assign dates they rely directly or indirectly on other kinds of evidence. For Syro-Palestinian pottery this usually means written records, and for Palestinian Iron Age pottery, the Hebrew Bible plays a major role in the process. Consider, for example, the famous 'collared-rim jar'. Is there anything about its shape or form that cries out 12th–11th century BCE? Of course not. Albright identified this ceramic type at Tell el-Fûl, which he believed to be Gibeah of Benjamin, and dated the jars accordingly. They have since turned up at other sites and in contexts that confirm his dating. But at these other sites also, the confirmation relies ultimately on written records, including the Hebrew Bible.

Summary and Conclusion

While it is theoretically possible to write a history of early Israel without relying on the Hebrew Bible, the result would be a very thin volume indeed and would have little in common with the current discussion. Any time historians, archaeologists, sociologists, or whoever speak of Israelite tribes settling the central Palestinian hill country during Iron I or of any sort of Israelite monarchy before the 9th century BCE, they are assuming information derived from the Hebrew Bible. The important question is not whether we should use the Hebrew Bible in our attempts to understand the origin and early history of Israel, but how we should use it. In my opinion, it should be approached critically, examined with the same careful attention to its internal typology and stratigraphy that archaeologists give to their data, and then used very cautiously, alongside other kinds of evidence, always with a conscious effort to avoid excessive circular argumentation. This process involves judgment calls every step of the way and will never lead to scientifically provable conclusions. But such is the nature of historiography.

ARCHAEOLOGY, MATERIAL CULTURE AND THE EARLY MONARCHICAL PERIOD IN ISRAEL

William G. Dever

From the beginnings of the 'biblical archaeology' movement it was assumed that archaeology would 'revolutionize' our knowledge of the biblical world, ancient Israel in particular. Recently, however, as the newer 'secular' discipline of Syro-Palestinian archaeology and various modern schools of biblical interpretation have increasingly diverged, skeptical voices on both sides appear to dominate the scene.[1] What *can* archaeology and biblical scholarship—that is, artifactual and textual studies—contribute to each other?

This paper will examine three areas of potential interaction between the two classes of data, focusing on the 10th–8th centuries BCE and choosing a few 'case studies' for each. (1) A re-examination of the older style *political history* will be perhaps largely negative, since it shows, for instance, how problematic various reconstructions of the Davidic-Solomonic era are becoming. (2) More positive will be the results from a survey of the archaeological data that now correlate with recent studies of the rise of the Israelite state, such as works by Flanagan, Frick, Lemche, Thompson, and others. Here, the pertinent case studies are the early Israelite and Judean capitals and regional centers: Jerusalem, Dan, Samaria, and Lachish. (3) It will be argued, however, that the most fruitful dialogue between archaeology and

---

1.   For recent treatments of the 'new archaeology' and of current developments in biblical and Syro-Palestinian archaeology, with full references, see W.G. Dever, 'The Impact of the "New Archaeology" on Syro-Palestenian Archaeology', *BASOR* 242 (1981), pp. 15-29; *idem*, 'Syro-Palestinian and Biblical Archaeology', in *The Hebrew Bible and its Modern Interpreters* (ed. D.A. Knight and G.M. Tucker; Philadelphia: Fortress Press, 1985), pp. 31-74; *idem*, 'Biblical Archaeology: Death and Rebirth?' (forthcoming in the Congress Volume of the Second International Congress of Biblical Archaeology in Jerusalem in June, 1990).

textual studies in the future may be in the area of religion and cult. A review of the evidence of shrines and temples from the 10th-8th centuries BCE will include data from Dan, Megiddo, Ta'anach, Tell el-Far'ah/Tirzeh, Lachish, Arad, and Kuntillet 'Ajrûd. In conclusion, it may be helpful to offer a few observations on the task facing the historian of ancient Israel, whether text scholar or archaeologist.

1. *Regional Centers*

Recent excavations in Jerusalem, the capital from early monarchical times onward and the focus of much of the biblical tradition as it has come down to us, have been seen by some as corroborating biblical historiography. One may note, especially from the work of the late Yigal Shiloh, the general illumination of the location and style of the Solomonic Temple, if not the discovery of any actual traces of the structure itself; the recovery of the stepped stone *millo* to the south and several fine residences of the elite quarter; hundreds of 'Asherah' figurines, right in the shadow of the Temple mount; and especially the hoard of clay *bullae* from the late 7th century BCE 'Burnt House' containing many names of royal and priestly individuals mentioned in the Bible.[1] One may note also the 7th century silver amulet from Ketef Hinnom, inscribed with a quotation of the 'priestly blessing' from Num. 6.24-26, our oldest surviving fragment of Hebrew Scripture by centuries.[2]

In summary, thus far in the archaeology of Jerusalem, there is nothing that is at variance with the biblical accounts. Nevertheless, I must point out that, here, archaeological artifacts neither corroborate nor correct the biblical text as it stands; they simply illuminate certain details. That is to be expected because the biblical tradition is centered in Jerusalem and ought to reflect the situation there.

Elsewhere in Israel, however, one of the proudest achievements of 'biblical archaeology'—the supposed recovery of nearly identical 'Solomonic' city walls, gateways and monumental architecture at

1.   See especially Y. Shiloh, *Excavations at the City of David*. I, 1978–82. *Interim Report of the First Five Seasons.* (Qedem, 19; Jerusalem: Institute of Archaeology, The Hebrew University of Jerusalem, 1984); and 'A Group of Hebrew Bullae from the City of David', *IEJ* 36 (1986), pp. 16-38.

2.   See G. Barkay, *Ketef Hinom. Burial Treasure from Jerusalem* (Israel Museum Catalogue, 274; Jerusalem: Israel Museum, 1986).

Hazor, Megiddo and Gezer—has come under sustained attack by several Israeli archaeologists who want to date all those remains to the 9th century BCE despite defences of the Solomonic date by John Holladay, Lawrence Stager, and myself.[1] At the other end of the spectrum, the raising of the date of the destruction of Lachish III by over a hundred years to 701 BCE has thrown the archaeological chronology and history of the late monarchy and the 7th century BCE into chaos.[2]

If we cannot assign anything archaeological to the age of David and Solomon, and not much of significance even to the days of Josiah, where does that leave us? Archaeology's potential for real *history-writing*, the very *foundation* of the 'biblical archaeology' movement, would seem to be threatened—and, I hasten to say, not by renegades like myself, but by younger *Israeli* scholars, whom many still suppose to be 'biblical archaeologists' in the classic mode of Albright and Wright. (I have shown, however, in the recently published Yadin *Festschrift* that this has never actually been true).[3] In any case, reports of the demise of Solomon are premature.

Let us take a second 'case study', the excavations at Tel Dan. Over the last 20 years, Avraham Biran has brought to light what was clearly the pre-Omride religious center of northern Israel, although biblical historians seem to have paid scant attention. Here I would simply mention the lower and upper city gates with their fine cobbled plazas and streets and especially the monumental 'High Places'. Here we have not only a huge open-air podium of Phoenician-style masonry, but an olive-pressing installation, horned altars, both animal and human figurines, and a subsidiary multiroomed shrine with its own altar, a *favissa* for sacrificial remains, several bronze shovels, and a splendid bronze scepter, no doubt for priestly usage. I would unequivocally identify these 9th–8th century BCE cultic installations with the 'High Place' (*bêt bāmôt*) first constructed by Jeroboam I, and

1. See *BASOR* 277-78 (1990); the Solomonic date is defended in the articles by I. Finkelstein, D. Ussishkin, and G.J. Wightman. For the methodological issues, see my reply, 'Of Myths and Method', *BASOR* 277-78 (1990), pp. 121-30.

2. See D. Ussishkin, 'Excavations at Tel Lachish, 1973–1977', *Tel Aviv* 5 (1978), pp. 1-97; *idem*, 'Excavations at Tel Lachish, 1978–1983', *Tel Aviv* 10 (1983), pp. 97-175.

3. See W.G. Dever, 'Yigael Yadin. Prototypical Biblical Archaeologist', *Eretz Israel* 20 (1989; the Yadin volume), pp. 44*-51*.

described in 1 Kgs 12.31. If so, then the archaeological record at Tel
Dan coincides perfectly with the admittedly tendentious denunciation
of the shrine of Dan by the deuteronomic historians, for the cult here
in the north was still identified with the old fertility religions of Late
Bronze Age Canaan.[1] At least, the archaeological data help to confirm
the bias of the Yahwistic writers of biblical tradition; at most, these
data *may* enable us to begin to write a more balanced 'history' of the
northern kingdom. That is a substantial, if hitherto largely unappreciated, achievement of recent archaeology.

I will not take time here to review the well-known discoveries at the
later capital of Samaria, for here again the archaeological record
seems to vindicate the ability of the biblical writers to record the
details of history in a factual manner[2]—when they *chose* to do so,
which is an absolutely fundamental distinction for the issues we are
discussing here.

I turn now to a final regional center of the monarchy, Lachish.
David Ussishkin's discoveries since 1973 have brilliantly recaptured
the archaeological setting of the fall of Lachish (Level III) to
Sennacherib in 701 BCE, as depicted both on his famous palace reliefs
now in the British Museum and in his *Annals*. Everything is here,
much of it now visible even to the casual tourist, in the current
reconstruction of the site: the breached and burnt lower and upper
city walls and gateway; the Assyrian siege ramp; and the pathetic, last-
minute counterramp thrown up inside the city. Even the intrepid
archaeologist, unsentimental as always, stands atop the mound at this
point and shudders, identifying with the doomed defenders of the city
on the eve of its destruction. This tragedy Sennacherib would cele-

---

1. On the finds from Dan, see conveniently A. Biran, 'Tel Dan Five Years
Later', *BA* 43 (1980), pp. 168-82; *idem*, 'The Dancer from Dan, the Empty Tomb
and the Altar Room', *IEJ* 36 (1986), pp. 168-78. For the continuity of early Israelite
religion with the Late Bronze Age Canaanite cult, see W.G. Dever, 'The
Contribution of Archaeology to the Study of Canaanite and Israelite Religion', in
Ancient Israelite Religion: Essays in Honor of Frank Moore Cross (ed. P.D. Miller,
P.D. Hanson and S.D. McBride; Philadelphia: Fortress Press, 1987), pp. 337-52.

2. On Samaria, see conveniently N. Avigad, 'Samaria', in *Encyclopedia of
Archaeological Excavations in the Holy Land*, IV (4 vols.; ed. M. Avi-Yonah and
E. Stone; Jerusalem: Massada Press 1978), pp. 1032-50. Add now P.J. King,
Amos, Hosea, Micah—An Archaeological Commentary (Philadelphia: Westminster
Press, 1988), pp. 36, 37, 65-69.

brate by dedicating a whole room of his palace back at Nineveh to the battle scenes.[1] From the viewpoint of the modern historian interested in the actual course of events, the fall of Lachish was probably the most portentous single happening of Judahite history in the closing years of the 8th century BCE. Yet this event is not even *mentioned* by the biblical writers, except that the writer of Kings notes in passing that Hezekiah sent messengers to Sennacherib at Lachish, the Chronicler adding that the city was under siege.

Why this silence? Obviously, from the deuteronomists' perspective, all that mattered was Yahweh's miraculous deliverance of Jerusalem, the capital, and its temple. Even here, however, there are serious inadequacies in the biblical account—not simply oversights, but misrepresentations, for the biblical writers *should* have possessed much the same information that we have now recovered from extrabiblical sources. Yet at one point, the biblical writers date the siege to 714 BCE. They also have the Egyptian Pharoahs wrong. The fact that Sennacherib succeeded in seizing forty-six towns in Judah—or, for that matter, that, as he put it, he shut up Hezekiah in Jerusalem 'like a bird in a cage'—is only hinted at in 2 Kgs 18-20 and 2 Chron 29-32. Finally, the biblical writers explain Jerusalem's salvation as due to Yahweh's sending a plague that devastated the Assyrian camp, killing 185,000 troops. The Assyrian version, on the other hand, suggests that Sennacherib was suddenly called back to Nineveh to put down an attempted *coup d'état*. The Bible has him killed forthwith by his two sons, but he died 20 years later. Given the obvious divergence of the two accounts, which is correct, if either? Or, to put it more precisely, which yields a superior history—a better documented, more nuanced reconstruction of what may actually have transpired? Which ultimately yields the most satisfying set of probabilities? Where the evidence is inadequate, that is probably all the historian can hope for.

In the case of Lachish III, however, archaeology issues a radical challenge to biblical historiography, for it supplies *much* more information than the Bible. One cannot sidestep that challenge by insisting that we simply have two differing but complementary versions of

---

1. See Ussishkin, 'Excavations, 1973–1977', and 'Excavations, 1978–1983'. A lavish republication of the Lachish reliefs, with newly executed drawings, has been done by D. Ussishkin (*The Conquest of Lachish by Sennacherib* [Tel Aviv: Institute of Archaeology, 1982]).

what really took place. Nor is it especially helpful to invoke the old, rather feeble 'two campaign theory'.[1] Rather, the historian is forced to evaluate (and perhaps to choose between?) two entirely distinct categories of data and indeed, two approaches to history-writing: one based exclusively on biblical sources and one based on the combination of texts from all sources, plus artifacts.

Fundamental to our task as this dilemma is, biblical historians have yet to face up to it, it seems to me. Witness the recent *History* by Miller and Hayes, which does not even mention the archaeological evidence for the fall of Lachish except to say that the correlation of stratum III with Sennacherib's campaign in 701 BCE is 'not certain'.[2] Postmodern, liberated scholars though we may be, we all tend to capitalize upon archaeology's discoveries when they seem to reinforce the biblical tradition (or, at least, our own interpretation of it) but to ignore these discoveries when they prove inconvenient.

As I have observed before, the 'archaeological revolution' in biblical history that Albright foresaw has come at last, but it may have sobering consequences. The 'new archaeology' may be, in fact, far more revolutionary than anyone has yet grasped—*if* we give it a chance.

I would argue that archaeological discoveries are already literally *forcing* us to rewrite the entire history of ancient Israel, from the so-called conquest to the exile and return. Yet if those of us who specialize in material culture and others who do texts cannot or are not willing to engage in serious and sustained dialogue, we are in for a disaster. We may ultimately produce *two* contradictory histories: (a) a 'history of ancient Palestine' based largely upon archaeological remains and emphasizing settlement history, technology, socio-economic structure, and cultural change; and (b) a 'history of Israelite religion', based almost exclusively on the texts of the Hebrew Bible

---

1. Thus, for instance, J. Bright, *A History of Israel* (London: SCM Press, 1960), pp. 282-87.
2. See J.M. Miller and J.H. Hayes, *A History of Ancient Israel and Judah* (Philadelphia: Westminster Press, 1986), p. 226. This is an astonishingly minimalistic statement—especially when one considers that Max Miller has done a good deal of fieldwork and has written on archaeological subjects. Yet one finds throughout this *History* virtually no use of modern archaeological results. In that respect, the work is a disappointment, indeed an anachronism.

(and, I might add, elaborated largely from the perspective of the Yahwist writers).

To be sure, the dilemma itself is recognized by a few of us on the archaeological side, as well as by several recent biblical historiographers of the socioanthropological school. I would single out among the latter (for their courage, if nothing else) Gottwald, Chaney, Coote and Whitelam, Flanagan, Frick, Van Seters, Halpern, Lemche, Garbini and Thompson.[1] These and other scholars have acknowledged that we are at an impasse, that we have reached the limits of traditional inquiries into Israel's remote or even more recent past. We confront an epistemological crisis that may well mark, after a century or more of progress, a radical departure for modern critical biblical scholarship. At issue is nothing less than our capacity to grasp the very nature of the early biblical community and of the characteristically theocentric way in which it rendered an account of itself (for that is what 'history' is). In short, can we ever hope to penetrate behind the later tradition to the full reality of ancient Israel in all its diversity, to its unique material and spiritual origins? What *is* this elusive *élan vital* that has shaped so much of our own experience and destiny; and why does it hold us moderns—whether Jews, Christians, or secularists—in such a 'state of psychological subjection' (as Garbini puts it)?[2]

---

1. See N.K. Gottwald, *The Tribes of Yahweh: A Sociology of Liberated Israel, 1250–1050 BCE* (Maryknoll, NY: Orbis Books, 1979); M.L. Chaney, 'Ancient Palestinian Peasant Movements and the Formation of Premonarchic Israel', in *Palestine in Transition. The Emergence of Ancient Israel* (SWBAS, 2; ed. D.N. Freedman and D.F. Graf; Sheffield: Almond Press, 1983), pp. 39-90; J. Van Seters, *In Search of History. Historiography in the Ancient World and the Origins of Biblical History* (New Haven: Yale University Press, 1983); F.S. Frick, *The Formation of the State in Ancient Israel* (SWBAS, 4; Sheffield: Almond Press, 1985); N.P. Lemche, *Early Israel. Anthropological and Historical Studies on the Israelite Society before the Monarchy* (VTSup, 37; Leiden: Brill, 1985); R.B. Coote and K.W. Whitelam, *The Emergence of Early Israel in Historical Perspective* (SWBAS, 2; Sheffield: Almond Press, 1983); J.W. Flanagan, *David's Social Drama. A Hologram of Israel's Early Iron Age* (SWBAS, 7; Sheffield: Almond Press, 1988); G. Garbini, *History and Ideology in Ancient Israel* (trans. J. Bowden; New York: Crossroad, 1988); B. Halpern, *The First Historians: The Hebrew Bible and History* (New York: Harper & Row, 1988); T.L. Thompson, *The Origin Tradition of Ancient Israel* (JSOTSup, 55; Sheffield: JSOT Press, 1987).

2. Garbini, *History and Ideology*, p. 174; cf. also pp. 1-20.

2. *Religion and Cult*

Upon much reflection, I have come to think that it is in the area of
religion and cult (including perhaps a reinvestigation of the very
foundations of 'biblical' and even systematic theology) that we will
find the most fruitful dialogue between archaeologists and historians
of Israel and Judah in the near future. Recent archaeological discoveries bearing upon the cult in the Iron Age or Israelite period are
incredibly rich and exciting, but here I can only highlight the main
points.[1]

1. The 12th century BCE 'Bull Site' of Amihai Mazar appears to
    be an authentic Israelite tribal sanctuary in the territory of
    Manasseh, dedicated to Yahweh but strongly reminiscent of
    Canaanite El, whom the Bible acknowledges as 'the god of
    the fathers' (as Cross and others had already demonstrated).[2]

2. Israelite private and household shrines of the 12th–10th cen-
    turies BCE at Beth-Shan, Megiddo, Ta'anach, Tell
    Far'ah/Tirzeh, 'Ai, Lachish, and elsewhere—some known
    for a generation or more—have yielded numerous horned
    incense altars, terra-cotta offering stands, model temples,
    exotic cult vessels, hundreds of 'Asherah' figurines, and other
    ritual paraphernalia that illuminate early Israelite religious
    practice before the establishment's attempt to unify and cen-
    tralize worship in Jerusalem in the 8th–7th centuries BCE.
    The finds probably even predate the period when Israelite
    religion began to develop toward the lofty 'ethical mono-
    theism' that the later deuteronomic and prophetic texts
    regard as normative.[3]

3. Israelite Ta'anach in the 10th century BCE—exactly contem-
    porary with the founding of the Solomonic royal cult in

1.   For the most convenient recent surveys, see Dever, 'Contribution of Archae-
ology'; J.S. Holladay, 'Religion in Israel and Judah under the Monarchy: An
Explicitly Archaeological Approach', in *Ancient Israelite Religion* (ed. P.D. Miller,
P.D. Hanson and S.D. McBride), pp. 249-99.

2.   See A. Mazar, 'The "Bull Site": An Iron Age I Open Cult Place', *BASOR*
247 (1982), pp. 27-42.

3.   See Dever, 'Contribution of Archaeology'; and especially Holladay,
'Religion in Israel and Judah'.

Jerusalem—reveals a public sanctuary with an oil-pressing installation, a hoard of astragali for divination, and a mold for mass producing 'Asherah' mother-goddess figurines. In addition, there is an absolutely astonishing piece of early Israelite iconography: a large offering stand that depicts on the bottom register a smiling, nude Asherah—well attested in ancient Canaan as 'the Lion Lady'—grasping two lions by the ears. (Another fantastic lion stand was found nearby by German excavators 75 years ago and is now in Istanbul).[1]

4. The recent publications of Iron Age Tell el-Far'ah (N), the early Israelite capital of Tirzeh, have brought to light a thus far unique 10th century BCE Israelite *näos* or household model temple. Nearly all the non-Israelite examples of *naoi* are associated with lions and/or doves, clearly symbols of Asherah/Tanit in the Canaanite–Phoenician world. There are also a gate shrine, an oil press, and numerous cultic figurines at Israelite Far'ah.[2]

5. Still more remarkable is the full-scale 10th(?)–8th century BCE Israelite sanctuary found by Aharoni at Arad (inadequately dug and published, however, and thus still unappreciated by most biblical scholars). Here we actually have a full-fledged tripartite temple, built on the same basic plan as that in Jerusalem. It features a large outer altar for animal sacrifice; a central room (*hêkāl*), with two smaller incense altars flanking the far doorway; and an inner chamber (*d^ebîr*), with a large stela (*massēbâ*). At the base of the large outer altar there have been found, among other items, charred animal bones; two offering plates inscribed in Hebrew with *gōp kaph*, that is, 'set apart for the priests'; terra cotta offering stands; and still another hint of Asherah, a fine bronze lion.[3]

1. See W.G. Dever, 'Asherah, Consort of Yahweh? New Evidence from Kuntillet 'Ajrud', *BASOR* 255 (1984), pp. 29-37; R. Hestrin, 'The Lachish Ewer and the Asherah', *IEJ* 37 (1987), pp. 212-23.

2. On the *naos*, see A. Chambon, *Tell el-Far'ah. I. L'age du fer* (Paris: Editions Recherche sur les Civilisations, 1984), pl. 66; cf. other *naoi* in S.S. Weinberg, 'A Moabite Shrine Group', *Muse* 12 (1978), pp. 30-48.

3. See for example. Z. Herzog, M. Aharoni, A.F. Rainey and S. Moshkovitz, 'The Israelite Fortress at Arad', *BASOR* 254 (1984), pp. 1-34; but note the radical

6.   Easily the most provocative cult site recently brought to light is Kuntillet 'Ajrûd, an 8th century BCE Israelite shrine in the eastern Sinai desert. 'Ajrûd has produced a number of startling finds: dozens of Hebrew inscriptions, some invoking blessing in the names of El and Baal alongside Yahweh; votive offerings of various kinds; fragments of textiles that look like tapestries; and a number of store jars with painted scenes that depict the main themes of much older Canaanite art and iconography. One such scene features a half-nude female, seated on the lion throne that is often associated with deities in the Canaanite–Phoenician world. I have suggested that the 'Lady of 'Ajrûd' is Asherah. At this site she may even have been conceived of as the consort of Yahweh, for a Hebrew inscription just above this scene mentions 'Yahweh and *his* Asherah' in a blessing formula.[1] The two are mentioned together again in the 8th century tomb inscription from el-Qôm in the Hebron hills, which I published 20 years ago.[2] *Despite* problems of linguistic and art-historical interpretation, this (and much other) new evidence of the persistence of the cult of Asherah—whoever or whatever the Hebrew term connotes—must be faced, and histories of Israelite religion must be rewritten accordingly.[3]

adjustment of dates with which I fully concur in D. Ussishkin, 'The Date of the Judaean Shrine at Arad', *IEJ* 38 (1988), pp. 142-57.

1.   For the 'Ajrûd material, see Z. Meshel, 'Did Yahweh Have a Consort? The New Religious Inscriptions from Sinai', *BARev* 5/1 (1979), pp. 24-34; P. Beck, 'The Drawings from Ḥorvat Teiman (Kuntillet 'Ajrud)', *Tel Aviv* 9 (1982), pp. 3-86; and cf. the early attempt at synthesis in Dever, 'Consort of Yahweh?'. The literature is now proliferating too much to cite in full, but for the belated impact on historians of ancient Israel, see the various comments of Coogan, McCarter, Miller, and Tigay in *Ancient Israelite Religion* (ed. P.D. Miller, P.D. Hanson and S.D. McBride).

2.   See W.G. Dever, 'Iron Age Epigraphic Material from the Area of Khirbet el-Kôm', *HUCA* 40-41 (1970), pp. 139-204. Add now Z. Zevit, 'The Khirbet el-Qôm Inscription Mentioning a Goddess', *BASOR* 255 (1984), pp. 39-47; Hestrin, 'Lachish Ewer', both with literature in intervening years. Cf. also Dever, 'Consort of Yahweh?'.

3.   For the best, most recent 'state-of-the-art' survey, see Miller, Hanson, and McBride (eds.), *Ancient Israelite Religion*—although several of the text-based treatments are disappointing conventional.

None of the accumulating archaeological data regarding the cult should be disconcerting; the evidence simply confirms what biblical scholars have long suspected, namely that Yahwism in ancient Israel was *far* more syncretistic than the idealized portrait of the literary sources in the Hebrew Bible would have us believe. In short, the theological bias of the deuteronomistic sources and the liturgical preoccupations of the priestly sources must be supplemented and balanced by recourse to the prophetic strand of the tradition, which reminds us how prevalent the old fertility cults of Canaan remained. In particular, archaeology—which is uniquely capable of illuminating 'folk religion'—must now be brought into the picture (i.e. individual cult practice, as perhaps opposed to state-sponsored religious practices).

Yet positivist histories of Israelite religion are still being written that stress *ideology*, both ancient and modern, at the expense of actual religious practice, which we are now finally in a position to grasp, thanks to modern archaeological discoveries. It is the archaeological data alone that provide a witness that is 'external' to the biblical texts and thus offer an invaluable corrective. Artifactual evidence may not take precedence over texts in the task of historical reconstruction, but the two sources of data are often of equal value. Above all, archaeological data can no longer be ignored or dismissed by the biblical historian as 'mute' or inferior to texts because of problems of interpretation.[1]

3. Conclusion

I cannot resist a few pertinent (or perhaps impertinent) observations on the relative utility of texts and artifacts in history writing. Some biblical historians have apparently been mesmerized by texts, as though they offer a direct and incontrovertible insight into the 'actual realities' of the past. This seems to me an incredibly naïve view of the written word, indeed of language itself. Frake has pointed out that

---

1.   On the relation of artifacts to texts in history writing, see my forthcoming papers 'Unresolved Issues in the Early History of Israel: Toward a Synthesis of Archaeological and Textual Reconstructions' (in the Gottwald *Festschrift*, forthcoming); and 'Archaeology, Texts, and History-writing': Toward an Epistemology' (in the H.N. Richardson *Festschrift*, forthcoming).

language is simply a 'finite, shared code, the code being a set of rules for the socially appropriate construction and interpretation of messages'.[1] Thus texts—exactly like artifacts—are merely symbols of how people perceived reality, not exact descriptions of what 'really happened'. To go a step further, Lévi-Strauss observes that 'language can be said to be a condition of culture because the material out of which language is built is of the same type out of which the whole culture is built'.[2] That is to say, all texts are *culturally* conditioned, not 'objective' reports at all.

A similar way of assessing the value of texts would be to use Pike's famous 'emic–etic' distinction. *Emic* (as in 'phonemic') is structural, or society and culture as they really function and understand themselves; but *etic* (as in 'phonetic') is non-structural, or the analysis of society by others.

In this view, history writing is then merely the 'grammar' that we moderns devise and employ, somewhat arbitrarily, in order to analyze the language of the past. However skillful we may be as linguists, we are not 'native speakers' of the dead language and we can never penetrate fully the mystery that is portrayed symbolically. That is just as true of the interpretation of texts as of artifacts. Both texts and artifacts are symbolic expressions; a reflection as well as a refraction of shared experience; 'encoded messages' about how the human past was perceived, which we must try to decode before we can hope to understand 'how it was' in the past.

And, finally, what *is* 'history': what tradition says, or what the majority of people did? Who knows best what events 'mean': the original actors and participants, or later commentators? What is trivial and what is significant, in the long run? And, where ideology and religion are concerned, as in any reconstruction of ancient Israelite life, how can we determine what is 'normative' and thereby compelling? These are questions we must *all* ponder before we attempt to do history.

Max Miller asks, 'Is it possible to write a history of early Israel without relying on the Hebrew Bible?' Of course it is—or at least of

    1.   C. Frake, 'Notes on Queries in Ethnography', *American Anthropologist* 66.2.3 (1964), p. 133.
    2.   C. Lévi-Strauss, *Structural Anthropology* (New York: Basic Books, 1969), pp. 68, 69.

early Iron Age Palestine, including Israel. It all comes down finally to this: what kind of history do we *want*, and what kind will our sources allow?

> 'Thick' or 'thin'?
> Episodic or continuous (like Braudel)?
> Public or private?
> Elitist or popular?
> Political or socioeconomic?
> Ideological or descriptive?
> Dynamic or static?

Each generation must write its own history of ancient Israel, for its own purposes. Let ours benefit from the powerful new tool of archaeology, which alone promises to penetrate behind the tradition to recover at least part of the original events that have been lost to us in transmission. Only in that way can we hope to grasp the reality of ancient Israel in all its materiality and spirituality.[1]

Tolstoy once observed that historians are deaf men, seeking to answer questions that no one is asking. How often have we been deaf, both to the concerns of those who lived in ancient Israel and in our own world, so remarkably similar in the crises it faces; preoccupied with sterile, academic inquiries that imprison us in historicism? We can be liberated only by combining archaeological and textual studies in a dialogue that is dynamic—constantly open to new data and to new insights. Only thus are we likely to find a more satisfying portrait of early Israel.

---

1. Gottwald, *Tribes of Yahweh*, p. xxv.

THE ROLE OF ARCHAEOLOGICAL AND LITERARY REMAINS IN RECONSTRUCTING ISRAEL'S HISTORY[1]

Gösta W. Ahlström

Any person attempting an analysis of the history of the ancient Near East including ancient Israel and Judah is faced with so many problems that it often seems impossible to find out what history really looked like. History is the actual events, the empirical acts. With F. Braudel, we could say that history is very much concerned with 'man in his relationship to the environment',[2] which may even include changes in nature, natural or humanly contrived. As Braudel expressed it, we can 'dissect history into various planes'; that is, history can be divided 'into geographical time' ('man's relationship to the environment'), 'social time, and individual time'.[3]

Because not all of the empirical acts are known from documents, monuments or artifacts, we will never know the full story. Therefore, a presentation of the events and of humanity's involvement will, by necessity, include the use of hypotheses to fill the gaps in our knowledge. In other words, a presentation of the past becomes a reconstruction. That is what we call historiography. The two pillars we have upon which we may build a historical reconstruction are literary and archaeological remains. A historian can never be a textual scholar only, nor a pure archaeologist. However, a report of the actual events and facts does not really present history, that is, knowledge of the past. A report of the events will always be more or less incomplete. 'Knowledge requires some mode of viewing or arranging the events

---

1. I am indebted to Diana Edelman for valuable comments and for stylistically improving my English

2. F. Braudel, *The Mediterranean and the Mediterranean World in the Age of Philip II*, I (Evanston: Harper & Row, 1972), p. 20.

3. Braudel, *The Mediterranean*, pp. 20-21.

that happen.'[1] Since the archaeological material is not self-explanatory but needs to be interpreted, a certain subjectivity will always be present in both the evaluation of source material and in final reconstructions of events.

Every reconstruction of history requires the historian to weigh the reliability, importance and relative value of the available sources. Textual material can be classified into two groups, primary and secondary sources. The former group includes texts, usually written close to the event, such as chronicles, annals, contracts, law codes, treaty texts, letters, etc. Secondary literary sources include, for instance, copies of an original document or composition, re-editings or rewritings of earlier material, or falsifications of documents.

Archaeological remains are always primary sources. However, they are 'mute' so their dating and their interpretation will be problematic without accompanying written material. The less we know about the finds, the less objectivity there will be in our interpretation and dating, since we will tend to explain objects and relationships from our own cultural biases and experiences. Thus, archaeological material can also lend 'itself to misunderstanding of one form or another'.[2] However, we may find that recognizable tool marks on stones in a wall or a certain architectural style can give an approximate date. Differences in pottery and pottery forms can also lead to a fairly reliable date. Of utmost importance in excavating tells is a careful, detailed stratigraphical sequence. With a reliable method of interpretation, archaeology can confirm the interpretation of a text,[3] supplement it, contradict it, or revise the existing textual testimony; in addition it can provide information not found in any text. If the meaning of the archaeological evidence is clear, one might say that it gives a more 'neutral' history than the textual material. It is free from the *Tendenz* or evaluation that easily creeps into an author's writings. However, we can never write a complete history based on archaeological remains only. For certain periods we only have archaeological

1. J.W. Miller, *The Philosophy of History with Reflections and Aphorisms* (New York and London: Norton, 1981), p. 116.

2. A. Snodgrass, 'Archaeology', in *Sources for Ancient History* (ed. M. Crawford; Cambridge: Cambridge University Press, 1983), p. 137.

3. R. de Vaux, 'On Right and Wrong Uses of Archaeology', in *Near Eastern Archaeology in the Twentieth Century* (ed. J.A. Sanders; Garden City, NY: Doubleday, 1970), p. 78.

remains upon which to rely, and yet, because only certain areas and often only a small part of a tell has been archaeologically investigated, a history based on their remains is at best spotty.[1]

Biblical historiography is a literary phenomenon whose primary goal is not to create a record of factual events.[2] Rather, it is a form of writing steered by the writers' idea that the events being described were expressions of the divine will.[3] The biblical material has been organized thematically so that its ideological points come through.[4] In other words, biblical historiography is dogmatic in character. Therefore, a 'biblical historian' is a scholar who does not deal primarily with empirical events, but who analyzes the Bible's historiography. Because the authors of the Bible were historiographers and used stylistic patterns to create a 'dogmatic' and, as such, tendentious literature, one may question the reliability of their product. The Hebrew Bible is part of a common Near Eastern way of expressing events and ideas. Egyptian texts, for example, typically use a stylistic pattern whose aim is to glorify Egypt and/or the Pharaoh, who was always protecting the 'divine' realm, the nation, which 'had been entrusted' to him.[5] Since stylistic patterns are not made for rendering actual events, they are not always helpful in reconstructing history.

Methodologically a historian cannot interpret the archaeological material by first asking what the biblical text says. The character of these two types of sources is different. The data are different and so

---

1.   It would, for instance, be very difficult to establish ethnicity, because different ethnic groups could have had the same material culture; see, for instance, de Vaux, 'Right and Wrong Uses', p. 78, and G. London, 'A Comparison of Two Contemporaneous Lifestyles of the Late Second Millennium B.C.', *BASOR* 273 (1989), pp. 37-55.

2.   T.L. Thompson maintains that 'the biblical tradition is not a history at all' (*The Origin Tradition of Ancient Israel. The Literary Formation of Genesis and Exodus 1–23* [JSOTSup, 55; Sheffield: JSOT Press, 1987], p. 39).

3.   W.F. Albright stated that 'the ancient historiographer was seldom dishonest, but frequently the victim of his point of view' ('The Administrative Division of Israel and Judah', *JPOS* 5 [1925], p. 23).

4.   See, for instance, G. Savran, '1 and 2 Kings', in *The Literary Guide to the Bible* (ed. R. Alter and F. Kermode; Cambridge, MA: Belknap Press of Harvard University, 1987), pp. 146-64.

5.   J.A. Wilson, 'Egyptian Civilization', in *Propaganda and Communication in World History. I. The Symbolic Instrument in Early Times* (ed. H.D. Lasswell, D. Lerner and H. Speier; Honolulu: University Press of Hawaii, 1979), p. 145.

are their composition/construction. The biblical literary material is the product of a particular indoctrination and can be characterized as an ideological presentation that has used or even misused some of the facts. Only rarely was it intended to serve as the *legend* for explaining the origin or meaning of artifacts and building remains. In practice then, it will often be impossible to harmonize the archaeological sources with the biblical ones,[1] as has frequently been done. One could even ask whether a harmonization should be done. The results may be historically misleading.

In order to clarify the problems under discussion the following phenomena will be considered:

1.   Textual information steering the archaeological interpretation.
2.   Artifactual information for excavations widening the historical horizon.
3.   The conflict between textual advocacy and excavated facts.
4.   The purpose and reliability of the biblical historical texts.

1. *Textual Information Steering the Archaeological Interpretation*

As already mentioned, archaeological material is, in itself, problematic as long as it does not yield exact information about its time, function and origin. Thus, a certain subjectivity, in many cases inspired by the biblical texts, often steers its interpretation. This is particularly true for scholarly treatments of the early Iron I period, in which excavation results have in most instances been interpreted in light of biblical historiography.

Hazor provides a good example of how biblical historiographic construction has been used to explain how the destruction of a mighty city was to have resulted from invading nomads who were 'Israelites'.[2] The biblical construction of an 'Israelite conquest' of

---

1.   See A.E. Glock, 'Text and Archaeology at Tell Ta'annek', *Berytus* 31 (1983), p. 57. 'Digging up the Holy Land does not mean digging up the Bible', according to H.J. Franken ('The Problem of Identification in Biblical Archaeology', *PEQ* 108 [1976], p. 10).

2.   See, among others, Y. Yadin, *Hazor: The Head of all those Kingdoms, Joshua 11:10* (The Schweich Lectures of the British Academy, 1970; London: Oxford University Press, 1972), pp. 129-32; S.M. Paul and W.G. Dever, *Biblical*

Canaan has, as in so many other cases, furnished the method used to interpret the archaeological remains. The first Iron I stratum at Hazor (stratum XII), which was characterized by some pits and the remains of a few huts, has been labeled 'Israelite', even though there were no remains that clearly indicated who the people were who used the place, or their place of origin. There is no indication whatsoever for who the settlers of stratum XII were or if they ever settled there. One must state that the harmonization of archaeological remains and biblical texts in this case has been forced.

It is also with a certain skepticism that one learns about the periodization of strata XI-V at Hazor. These strata have been assigned according to different periods in the history of Israel.[1] Stratum XI would be the pre-Solomonic period, X Solomon's reign, IX the early 9th century BCE, VIII Ahab's rule, VII post-Ahab, VI Jeroboam II and Zechariah, VB Menahem, and VA would be the last Israelite city destroyed by Tiglath-pileser III in 732 BCE. All this could be right, but one just wonders with what archaeological method the excavators have managed to assign some buildings and strata to certain kings but not to others. For instance, both Jeroboam I and Baasha might have been interested in fortifying Hazor because of the danger that the Aramaean kingdom of Damascus represented. My point is that the archaeological remains have been 'speaking' through the Bible, not by themselves. Besides due consideration given to pottery and parallel architectural features at other sites, the dating of the strata has been 'inspired' by the biblical text.

The biblical invasion story and Josh. 8.30-31 has served as the basic inspiration for A. Zertal's interpretation of the building complex found on Mt Ebal. He has proposed that it was a cultic installation built by newly arrived 'Israelites'.[2] The site's status as a cult place is not the focus of our concern. What is important in our discussion and what is methodologically questionable is the excavator's reliance upon the biblical texts in order to 'establish' who built the structure. He has

Archaeology (New York: Quadrangle/The New York Times Book Co., 1974), p. 10.

  1.   See conveniently Y. Yadin, *Hazor: The Discovery of a Great Citadel of the Bible* (New York: Random House, 1975), pp. 274-75.

  2.   'An Early Iron Age Cultic Site on Mount Ebal: Excavation Seasons 1982–1987', *Tel Aviv* 13–14 (1986–87), pp. 105-65.

a priori accepted the biblical text as an accurate report of a historic event. His failure to recognize the ideological *Tendenz* of the literature weakens the reliability of his conclusions. When he also maintains that his reconstructed altar does not correspond to the configuration of other Israelite altars,[1] he has weakened his own argument.

These examples show that the literary style of the textual material, as well as the aim of the biblical writers, has not been clearly understood or analyzed. Biblical historical constructions have been used as a guide for interpreting the results of the excavations. The underlying methodological fallacy in the examples cited above is that any kind of change in the material culture of the hills can reveal the presence of the Israelites, who should have been a new ethnic group invading and/or conquering the land. Regional and geographic differences, which could have forced the settlers to adjust to a new way of life, have been ignored.

2. Artifactual Information from Excavations:
Widening the Historical Horizon

Archaeology does not only illustrate or correct textual witnesses. Artifacts and building remains can often inform us about phenomena not mentioned in any text, thus giving a quite different picture than that commonly painted by text alone. However, we must also recognize that archaeology can be misused to interpret the course of history. The dating and destruction of a temple excavated within the fortress at Arad in the Negev exemplifies the ease with which the archaeological data have been used or misused to describe the religious history of the nation Judah. The Bible does not mention that Arad housed either a fortress or a temple during the monarchic period.[2] In this case, archaeology has widened our horizon by providing a glimpse of Judahite religion and military administration that was not presented by the biblical writers. Since a temple within a fortress would not have been a private sanctuary, but part of the royal

---

1. A. Zertal, 'Has Joshua's Altar Been Found on Mt Ebal', *BARev* 11.1 (1985), pp. 39-40.

2. The deuteronomistic historiographer would most probably have seen Arad—if he had known it—as belonging to the *bāmāā* category, i.e., those temples and sanctuaries that the kings had built in the country, 2 Kgs 18.4; cf. 23.19.

The Fabric of History

establishment, the religion practiced at Arad must have represented the official cult of the kingdom. The temple has the form of an ordinary house with a broadroom containing a niche, and a main hall or 'courtyard', with an altar. It has been assigned a construction date in stratum XI. While the temple is commonly dated to the 10th century BCE,[1] in his recent investigation of the stratigraphy, D. Ussishkin dates it somewhat later, to strata X-VIII,[2] which, in his opinion, is 'one building phase'.[3] Whatever stratigraphy one accepts, the temple seems to have been destroyed at the end of the 8th century BCE or in the early 7th century BCE.[4]

Textual information about the cultic reforms of Hezekiah and Josiah has been used to provide the reason for the temple's failure to be rebuilt in stratum VII. The sacrificial altar in the main hall is thought to have gone out of existence already in stratum VIII. Arad is thus supposed to have become a victim of cult centralization. The biblical account of the reforms of Hezekiah and Josiah has been used without hesitation to explain the changes at Arad, even if it is not certain what shape these reforms took in the actual flow of history. When we do not know exactly what caused the abolition of the altar and of the temple itself, we have to be open to all possibilities. Cultic reforms offer one working hypothesis, but not the only one. Another equally plausible approach to the issue would be to look at the military-political picture of the Negev in the last century of Judah's existence as a kingdom in order to seek a possible working hypothesis.

Sennacherib's Palestinian campaign in 701 BCE almost eradicated the nation of Judah from the map. Although King Hezekiah is depicted in the Bible to have been one of the 'greatest' kings of Judah, in reality he almost destroyed his kingdom. The Assyrian inscriptions report

1. Y. Aharoni, 'The Solomonic Temple, The Tabernacle and the Arad Sanctuary', in *Orient and Occident. C.H. Gordon Volume* (ed. H.H. Hoffner; AOAT, 22; Neukirchen–Vluyn: Neukirchener Verlag, 1973), pp. 1-8. For the stratigraphy, see now, Z. Herzog, M. Aharoni, A.F. Rainey and S. Moshkovitz, 'The Israelite Fortress at Arad', *BASOR* 254 (1984), pp. 1-34.

2. D. Ussishkin, 'The Date of the Judean Shrine at Arad', *IEJ* 38 (1988), pp. 151-56.

3. Thus also O. Zimhoni, 'The Iron Age Pottery of Tel 'Eton and its Relation to the Lachish, Tell Beit Mirsim and Arad Assemblages', *Tel Aviv* 12 (1985), pp. 85-86.

4. Ussishkin, 'Judean Shrine', pp. 151-55.

that forty-six cities and many fortresses and villages of Judah were taken and transferred by Sennacherib to the administration of his vassal kings of Philistia, Mitinti of Ashdod, Padi of Ekron, and Sillibel of Gaza.[1] Although details of the destruction of a country are often exaggerated in inscriptions, in the present instance the figure of forty-six cities is probably trustworthy because it is an exact figure. In addition, we know that scribes were regular personnel in military campaigns and were charged with the official task of counting and registering the spoil. The Assyrian records raise the question whether the fortress at Arad was taken and destroyed by Sennacherib's troops in 701 BCE. Because no names of fortresses are given in the Assyrian annals, we cannot arrive at a certain conclusion, but the destruction of stratum VIII might plausibly be related to Assyrian activity.[2] A third explanation for the destruction of fortress VIII can be proposed; Assyria may have had an 'ally' in its vassal Edom at this time.[3] This is also a period when the Edomites regained much territory in the Negev. According to Arad ostracon 40, they made threatening incursions into southern Judah.[4] It is possible that most of the Negev of the 7th century BCE became divided between the Edomites[5] and the

1. D.D. Luckenbill, *Ancient Records of Assyria and Babylonia*, II (Chicago: University of Chicago Press, 1927), § 240, pp. 19-20; A.L. Oppenheim in *ANET* (Princeton: Princeton University Press, 1951), p. 288. A bull inscription from Nineveh adds Ashkelon (Luckenbill, *Records*, § 312, p. 143.)

2. Thus, Y. Aharoni, 'The Negeb and the Southern Borders', in *The World History of the Jewish People. IV.1. The Age of the Monarchies: Political History* (ed. B. Mazar; vol. ed. A. Malamat; Jerusalem: Jewish History Publications, 1979), p. 299.

3. *ANET*, p. 287. See also N. Na'aman, 'Hezekiah's Fortified Cities and the *LMLK* Stamps', *BASOR* 261 (1986), p. 13.

4. See, for instance, the discussion in Na'aman, 'Hezekiah's Fortified Cities', pp. 13-14. This letter mentions 'the evil that the Edomites have done'. Its date is debated. D. Pardee assigns it to the second half of the 7th cent. BCE (*Handbook of Ancient Hebrew Letters* [Sources for Biblical Study, 15; Chico, CA: Scholars Press, 1982], p. 28). See also Helga Weippert, who emphasizes the Edomite influences in the Negev (*Palästina in vorhellenistischer Zeit* [Handbuch der Archäologie; München: Beck, 1988], p. 625).

5. The Edomite cult structure at Qitmit (Wâdi Qaṭṭamat), c. 10 km south of Arad, is another indicator; see I. Beit-Arieh, 'An Edomite Temple at Horvat Qitmit', *Qadmoniot* 19 (1986), pp. 72-79. This sanctuary has three parallel long-rooms that are open to a court, as is the case with some Nabatean temples; see R. Hachlili, 'The

Philistines, even though the Assyrian annal does not mention the formal ceding of towns to Edom, as it does for Philistia. This may be explained by the fact that the eastern Negev was not an urban area.

The Edomites could possibly have taken Arad during or after the Assyrian campaign of 701 BCE. If we look at the new stratum that was built (VIII) around this time, the layout is quite different than that of stratum VIII. An inner wall was added in the south and partly in the northwestern corner. The temple structure was completely covered with earth and thus deliberately put out of use. Much of the pottery is different from that of the earlier strata.[1] The store jar of the 'type associated with the *lmlk* stamps disappears',[2] which indicates a time around 700 BCE for the new stratum (VII).[3] All these factors might indicate that the rebuilding of the site was undertaken by a new group of people. Thus, as a hypothesis explaining the destruction of stratum VIII and the building of the new fortress (stratum VIII) at Arad, Edomite activity in the region as an Assyrian vassal can be suggested. In this case, the deliberate burial of the temple structure is plausibly explained by the need to diminish Yahweh's domain and assert

Architecture of Nabatean Temples', *EI* 12 (1975), pp. 95-106. Compare also N. Glueck, 'The Nabatean Temple of Quaṣr Rabbah', *AJA* 43 (1939), pp. 381-87.

1.   A systematic investigation, including a petrographic analysis, comparing Edomite pottery with that of 7th century southern Judah has not been undertaken. However, Edomite pottery has turned up, for instance, at Tel Malḥatah and at Tell el-Kheleifeh. See N. Glueck, 'Some Edomite Pottery from Tell el-Kheleifeh', *BASOR* 188 (1967), pp. 8-38; E. Stern, 'Israel at the Close of the Period of the Monarchy: An Archaeological Survey', *BA* 38 (1975), p. 45. According to H.G. Conrad and B. Rothenberg, there are only Edomite remains from the 8th and 7th centuries BCE at Tell el-Kheleifeh (*Antikes Kupfer im Timna-Tal* [Bochum: Vereinigung der Freunde con Kunst und Kultur im Bergbau, 1980], p. 213 n. 32). For the pottery of the Negev of the 8th–6th cent. BCE, consult G.O. Pratico, who shows that the pottery of the Negev of this period has affinities with pottery from Meṣad Hashavyāhū in the west to Buṣeirah, Tawīlân, Ḥisbân and Dhîbân in the east ('Nelson Glueck's 1938–1940 Excavations at Tell el-Kheleifeh: A Reappraisal', *BASOR* 259 [1985], pp. 1-32).

2.   Z. Herzog *et al.*, 'The Israelite Fortress at Arad', *BASOR* 254 (1984), p. 22. The abolition of the Temple is associated with the Josianic reform by Herzog *et al.*, p. 23.

3.   For the date of these stamps and for their origin in the Shephelah, see H. Mommsen, I. Perlman and J. Yellin, 'The Provenience of the *lmlk* Jars', *IEJ* 34 (1984), pp. 89-113.

Qaush's rule of the site.[1] Two alternative explanations for the destruction of Arad's temple are possible. One is based on the Bible alone and the other on the Assyrian annals and the Bible. Both involve the intuitive application of circumstantial evidence to mute artifactual remains.

If the above picture of Edomite activities in the Negev is accurate, it is possible that Arad could have been Edomite for a short time. Later, the fortress may have capitulated to a Judahite force, because the Elyashib ostraca are from the latest decades of the Judean monarchy and no destruction level has been registered from the period between 700 and 600 BCE. The fortress must therefore have become part of Judah again, probably during the decline of the Assyrian empire, or after its fall.

The discussion of the stratigraphy at Arad is a reminder of the imperfection of archaeological methods and of the uncertainty of interpreting mute sources. The reliability of archaeological material is just as questionable as the reliability of the textual material as long as we do not have a perfect method for dating.

The failure of the OT writer to mention Arad and its temple, the cultrooms at Megiddo[2] and Tell ed-Duweir, or the fortified way station at Kuntillet 'Ajrûd among other cultic sites is easily explained in terms of internal biblical evidence. The writer or 'historiographer' did not mention any specific sanctuaries outside of Jerusalem on principle, preferring to include all of them among the *bāmôt* of the kingdom for polemical reasons.[3] Arad was not an official sanctuary of

1. D. Ussishkin maintains that the destruction of the temple cannot be associated with any of the cultic reforms ('Judean Shrine', pp. 155-56).

2. For this, see now D. Ussishkin, 'Schumacher's Shrine in Building 338 at Megiddo', *IEJ* 39 (1989), pp. 149-72.

3. The so-called model (or miniature) shrines (known from Arad, Kamid el-Loz, Deir 'Alla, Tell el-Far'ah (N), Megiddo, Amman, Kerak, Balu'a, among other sites) could perhaps be seen as indications for the *bāmâ* sanctuary's architectural style. These shrines of clay have the form of one-room houses. On each side of the entrance, which is an opening, some have a capital in proto-aeolic style; see, for instance, H.G. May and M. Engberg, *Material Remains of the Megiddo Cult* (OIP, 26; Chicago: University of Chicago Press, 1935), p. 17, pls. XIII-XV; A. Chambon, *Tell el-Far'ah. I. 'âge du fer* (Paris: Editions Recherche sur les Civilisations, 1984), pp. 17-18 and pl. 66.1; R.H. Dornemann, *The Archaeology of Transjordan in the Bronze and Iron Ages* (Milwaukee: Milwaukee Public Museum, 1983), pp. 143-45 (with lit.).

the northern Kingdom, as were Bethel and Dan, against which the writer had to polemicize because of his hostility to the existence of the kingdom of Israel. To mention specific temples in the kingdom of Judah would have been to weaken his programmatic writings. Archaeology has, in these cases, increased our knowledge about religious phenomena.

Like the Arad temple, the historical background of the palace structure found at Ramat Rahel south of Jerusalem has been understood in the light of the biblical material. It has usually been identified with the *bt hhpšwt*, 'infirmary, house of death',[1] in 2 Chron. 26.21; cf. 2 Kgs 15.5. This Hebrew term refers to a separate building which, according to the text, King Uzziah used when he became leprous and could not fulfill his duties as regent. However, there is no indication in the text where this house was located,[2] so that the equation of the structure at Ramat Rahel with Uzziah's palace of confinement is no more than a suggestion.

3. *The Conflict between Textual Advocacy and Excavated Facts*

This part of the paper is related to the first point but tries to show how archaeological remains must be treated independently from the textual witness. Religious tendencies found in the historiography of the Hebrew Bible have often misguided the interpretation of certain archaeological finds.

An evaluation of the available archaeological and textual material that relates to the process of urbanization in the Iron Age period favors the giving of primary weight to the archaeological remains over the contradictory biblical testimony about the so-called institution of Levitical cities mentioned in Joshua 21 (cf. 1 Chron. 6). The 'Levitical list' can be characterized as a literary construction. A recent survey in which about seventy sites were investigated as possible candidates for Levitical cities has demonstrated the unreliability of Joshua 21 as a historical source.[3] All forty-eight cities that are men-

---

1. A Schoors, 'Literary Phrases', in *Ras Shamra Parallels*, I (Analecta Orientalia, 49; ed. L.R. Fisher; Rome: Pontifical Biblical Institute, 1972), p. 28.

2. For the time and the style of the structures, see Y. Yadin, 'The Archaeological Sources for the Period of the Monarchy', in *The Age of the Monarchies* (ed. A. Malamat), pp. 211-13.

3. J.L. Peterson, *A Topographical Survey of the Levitical 'Cities' of Joshua 21*

tioned did not exist before the monarchy was instituted. Some of them, such as Jutta, Eshtemoa and Jattir in Judah first came into existence during the period of the 10th–8th centuries BCE. 1 Kgs 9.16 maintains that Gezer was destroyed and its Canaanite population massacred by an Egyptian pharaoh, with the city then being given to Solomon as a wedding present. In this instance, the Bible itself provides contradictory evidence for the date of the institution of the Levitical cities. Excavations at Heshbon in Transjordan have not revealed any settlement during the 10th century BCE, assuming Heshbon is to be identified with modern Hisban. The conclusion to be drawn from the available textual and artifactual evidence is that the common theory describing the Levitical cities as a premonarchic institution or as a government agency of the United Monarchy is inaccurate.[1] In this case, archaeology cannot support the information in Joshua 21.

The biblical (and scholarly) 'dogma' that Yahweh never had a *paredros* has been nullified by the finds from Kuntillet 'Ajrûd, a desert station in northern Sinai dating from about 800 BCE.[2] The site can either be interpreted as a way station built by the kingdom of Judah, which had stretched its domain down into the northern Sinai peninsula at this time, or as a fortified way station built in no-man's-land[3] by those who trafficked the route from Gaza to the Gulf of Aqaba—by the Philistines, the Phoenicians, or the Israelites. Because of the drawings with the inscriptions about 'Yahweh of Shomeron (Samaria) and his Asherah/asherah' and 'Yahweh of Teman and his Asherah/asherah'[4] (Teman is a reference to eastern Edom, probably

---

and 1 Chronicles 6: Studies on the Levites in Israelite Life and Religion (THD dissertation, Seabury Western Theological Seminary, Evanston, IL, 1979).

1. See my *Royal Administration and National Religion in Ancient Palestine* (SHANE, 1; Leiden: Brill, 1982), pp. 51-56 (with lit.). According to N. Na'aman, the list of Levitical cities should be seen 'as an artificial "literary" composition' (*Borders and Districts in Biblical Historiography* [Jerusalem Biblical Studies, 4; Jerusalem: Simor, 1986], p. 236).

2. The pottery from this site has been dated to the 9th–8th centuries BCE by Z. Meshel ('Did Yahweh have a Consort? The New Religious Inscriptions from the Sinai', *BARev* 5 [1979], p. 34).

3. Thus Weippert, *Palästina in vorhellenistischer Zeit*, p. 617.

4. The wooden asherah was a symbol of the goddess, so we do not need to dismiss a reference to the goddess here.

the ridgeland north of Wâdi Feinan [Punon][1]), the first option would be to see the builder of the place to have been the government of Israel. This would be possible if its founding date were sometime before Jehu's *coup d'état* in 841 BCE. A less probable date would be the time during the reigns of Jehu and his successors Jehoahaz and Joash, when Israel's treaty with Tyre was nullified by the murders of the Omrides and when Israel was at the mercy of Aram–Damascus. Nonetheless, during the Omride period Israelite merchants and others, together with Phoenicians, could have taken the route down the coast and via Gaza, 'Ein Qudeirat and Kuntillet 'Ajrûd to reach Ezion-Geber. Another period when this route could have been accessible to the people of Israel would have been the reign of Jeroboam II, that is, in the first half of the 8th century BCE.

The Kuntillet 'Ajrûd graffiti tell us that Yahweh had a consort and that this had been the case ever since he left Edom. The existence of a *paredros* for Yahweh is not explicitly mentioned by the biblical writers.[2] We know, however, of the cult of Asherah in the temple of Solomon,[3] and in a literary investigation completed in 1963[4] I concurred with A.T. Olmstead's conclusion of 1931[5] that Yahweh had a

1.   For Teman as the name of a territory in eastern Edom, see R. de Vaux, 'Téman, ville ou région d'Edom?', *RB* 76 (1969), pp. 379-85. E.A. Knauf sees the name as a synonym for Edom itself ('Alter und Herkunft der edomitischen Königsliste Gen. 36, 31-39', *ZAW* 97 [1985], pp. 249-50). This is right, but in Hab. 3.3 where Teman (originally meaning 'south') is paralleled with Paran, which is in the western Edom, Teman may refer to another part of Edom.

2.   For most people the inscription was a surprise. For instance, the excavator, Z. Meshel, found it 'thoroughly blasphemous' ('Consort', p. 31). Meshel likes to see the consort phenomenon as having been introduced in Judah during the reign of Athaliah; thus Judah's religion would have been contaminated by an outsider ('Kuntillet 'Ajrud. An Israelite Religious Center in Northern Sinai', *Expedition* 20.4 [1978], pp. 50-54).

3.   It should be emphasized that a deity worshipped in the royal temple of a capital belonged to the official religion of the state. The scholarly treatment of this phenomenon, however, gives the impression that a beautiful Canaanite prostitute had sneaked into the temple of Yahweh.

4.   G.W. Ahlström, *Aspects of Syncretism in Israelite Religion* (Horae Soederblomianae, V; Lund: Gleerup, 1963), pp. 50-57.

5.   A.T. Olmstead, *History of Palestine and Syria to the Macedonian Conquest* (New York: Charles Scribner's Sons, 1931), pp. 298-99. Recently S.M. Olyan has advocated the same (*Asherah and the Cult of Yahweh* [SBLMS, 34; Atlanta: Scholars

consort. The material remains from Kuntillet 'Ajrûd have shown something about Israelite religion that the biblical writers tried to suppress.[1]

It has been common to maintain that the paintings and the inscription represent an expression of a popular form of the Israelite religion. That may be true, since we do not know in detail what popular religion was like at this time. However, I would maintain instead that the writings represent the official concept of the divine in the Northern Kingdom,[2] and I build this argument on the phrase 'Yahweh of Shomeron'. Whoever made these graffiti—a merchant or his servant, a priest from Israel, or a person passing by who decided to give some gifts to the gods—was an adherent of the official Yahweh cult of Samaria. Thus, his concepts would have been guided by the official religion. Furthermore, if the site had been built by Israelites—not Judahites, Phoenicians, or Philistines—it would have been an expression of the mercantile policy of the Northern Kingdom. In that kingdom Yahweh of Jerusalem did not have any power. It was not his land.

4. *The Purpose and Reliability of the Biblical Historical Texts*

Our task in trying to establish with some certainty the history of the peoples of the Hebrew Bible must begin with a realization about the character of the Hebrew Bible, and then with an attempt to find out by whom and for whom the textual material was written. Concerning the first point, it is evident that the Bible is a religious document, holy writ, and as such it does not really show any interest in rendering a faithful picture of history. Any sacred literature is by nature religious propaganda. It uses historical events as it sees fit. If the events do not fit the ideology of its writers, they can either be made to fit or ignored altogether.

Internal evidence in the books of Kings and the literary prophets shows that the Bible is presented from a Judahistic, Jerusalemite point

Press, 1988]).

1.   One could, therefore, maintain that Yahweh was no bachelor, but the biblical writers made him a widower.

2.   See also J.A. Emerton, who sees the text as an indication of a non-Jerusalemite Yahweh tradition ('New Light on Israelite Religion: The Implications of the Inscriptions from Kuntillet 'Ajrud', *ZAW* 94 [1982], pp. 2-20).

of view. The historiography reflects the ideology of a certain group in Judah who believed that the kingdom of Israel should never have existed as a separate kingdom, because it was 'sinful'. Its cardinal sin was to have split the United Monarchy. At the same time this polemical attitude defends the political supremacy of the kingdom of Judah. For this group, Jerusalem, with its Davidic dynasty and its form of Yahwistic religion, should have been the center for the northern people and not Bethel, which appears in the textual material as *the* cult place of the North. The unexpected prominence of Bethel can be explained in at least two ways. Jerusalemite circles may not have known much about the religious traditions of its northern neighbor, Israel. Alternatively, they might not have wanted to acknowledge them. Bethel and its traditions, however, became part of the Jerusalemite horizon in the days of King Josiah. He seems to have managed to increase his kingdom's territory by incorporating a small part of the Assyrian province of Samerina. This may be inferred from the fact that the border was just north of Bethel and Ai during the Persian period (Ezra 2.28).[1]

---

1. We may assume that the Babylonians and the Persians did not change the borders of the subprovinces; see J.M. Miller and J.H. Hayes, *A History of Ancient Israel and Judah* (Philadelphia: Westminster Press, 1986), p. 401. The common opinion that Josiah extended his kingdom by incorporating the Assyrian provinces of Magidu and Samerina is built on the passages 2 Kgs 23.15, 29 and 2 Chron. 34.6-7. F.M. Cross, for instance, thinks that Josiah would have intended to rebuild the Davidic kingdom 'in detail' (*Canaanite Myth and Hebrew Epic* [Cambridge, MA: Harvard University Press, 1973], p. 283). However, none of these texts gives any indication for such an expansion. See my article 'Prophetical Echoes of the Assyrian Growth and Decline', in *DUMU-E₂-DUB-BA-A. Studies in Honor of Åke W. Sjöberg* (ed. H. Behrens, D. Loding and M. Roth; Occasional Publications of the Samuel Noah Kramer Fund, 11; Philadelphia: Philadelphia University Museum, 1989), pp. 1-6. Also see my book, *The History of Ancient Palestine from the Palæolithic Period to Alexander's Conquest, with a Contribution by Gary O. Rollefson* (Sheffield: JSOT Press, forthcoming). Neither is there any indication that Josiah battled the Egyptian army under Necho II at Megiddo. It is also doubtful whether Josiah built the fortress Meṣad Hashavyāhū on the Philistine coast, as has been maintained. See the discussion by R. Wenning, 'Meṣad Hashavyāhū Ein Stützpunkt des Jojakim?', in *Vom Sinai zum Horeb Stationen alttestamentlicher Glaubensgeschichte. Festschrift Erich Zenger* (ed. F.-L. Hossfeld; Würzburg: Echter Verlag, 1989), pp. 169-96. Another possibility is that the fortress could have been the site of an Egyptian garrison to which Josiah and/or Jehoiakim had to send troops.

With the traditions of Bethel becoming part of the 'heritage' of the Southern Kingdom[1] the Jerusalemite literary elite could use them as a weapon against the Israelites in their propaganda against the North. Because of access to these traditions, Bethel's cult place became the representative for Jerusalem's concept of Israel in the religious competition with the North. This partly explains why we learn so little about Samaria's role as the center of the official northern form of the Israelite religion.[2] Consequently, the most important dynasty of the Northern Kingdom, that of the Omrides, is declared 'evil'. In other words, we get an 'upside-down' history of the kingdom of Israel. Among the Bethel traditions were, for instance, references to prophets who had had some association with the Bethel sanctuary, such as Amos, Hosea, Elijah and Elisha. The hostility to the people and religion of Israel found among the oracles of Amos and Hosea have been well utilized by the biblical compilers.[3] Other prophetic movements in the North are not mentioned, with the exception of a few prophetic individuals. The reason for this is that most prophets of the Northern Kingdom were not negative to their own nation. Thus, their oracles did not suit any ideology at home in Judah.[4]

A structural analysis of the books of Kings shows that the biblical historiographer has put his emphasis upon the period of the Omri dynasty, creating a narrative of fourteen chapters that is out of proportion with the account of the rest of the events in the Northern Kingdom.[5] The intention of the mastermind who composed this piece

1. D. Edelman has emphasized the importance of the Bethel and Gilgal traditions in the Jerusalemite historiography as a result of Josiah's annexation of southwestern Ephraim ('Boundaries and Deuteronomistic Source Materials' [paper presented Oct. 18, 1988 at the 289th meeting of the Chicago Society of Biblical Research]).

2. H. Tadmor, among others, has even maintained that Samaria was of no religious importance for the nation Israel ('On the History of Samaria in the Biblical Period', in *Eretz Shomron* [Jerusalem: Israel Exploration Society, 1972], pp. 67-69 [Hebrew]).

3. It is thus a methodological mistake to use Amos and Hosea as sources for religious and social phenomena in 8th century Israel. This may lead to exaggerations, such as John Bright's statement that Israel 'was inwardly rotten and sick past curing' (*A History of Israel* [3rd edn; Philadelphia: Westminster Press, 1981], p. 266).

4. The so-called end of prophecy can be explained in a similar way. After Malachi, no more 'suitable' prophets were taken into account. Prophecy did not die.

5. See Savran, '1 and 2 Kings', pp. 148-49. This history of the two kingdoms after the split to the fall of Israel comprises, in all, twenty-eight chapters

of literature has been twofold: to blame the Omri dynasty, and especially Ahab and Jezebel, for having introduced Baal worship[1] and to design its destruction with Elisha and Jehu. This intention makes the story quite propagandistic and must in turn create doubt about its reliability as a historical source. In this case history has been 'twisted' in order to suit a certain purpose. In this narrative cycle the *dramatis personae* are the prophets Elijah and Elisha and their opponents, the kings and Queen Jezebel.[2] Since the prophets are considered always to be right, the evaluation of the royal family is negative, and the real events of time are of less importance or of no interest to the writer. Realizing the writer's attitude, it is quite in order that no mention is made of such a historic event as the battle at Qarqar in 853 BCE, in which Ahab of Israel participated in a coalition against the Assyrian King Shalmaneser III. It did not suit the writer's purpose.[3]

In view of the foregoing considerations it is self-evident that we have no possibility of describing or analyzing with any accuracy the history of the religion of the kingdom of Israel. Archaeological remains from the areas of the Northern Kingdom would not, in principle, support the biblical evaluation of the religious phenomena and artifacts.[4] With the Bethel traditions being used freely by the

(1 Kgs 12–2 Kgs 17).

1. Naturally, no attempt has been made to differentiate between the imported Phoenician Baal and the indigenous Baal. See my *Royal Administration and National Religion in Ancient Palestine*, pp. 62-63.

2. Savran, '1 and 2 Kings', p. 149.

3. See my article, 'The Battle at Ramoth-Gilead in 841 BC', in *Wünschet Jerusalem Frieden* (ed. M. Augustin and K.-D. Schunck; Beiträge zur Erforschung des Alten Testaments und des antiken Judentums, 13; Frankfurt am Main: Peter Lang, 1988), p. 166.

4. The biblical denunciation of idols (for instance, Ashtarte figurines and bull figurines) cannot be used as a 'measuring rod' for right or wrong religious phenomena in the Northern Kingdom. The right or official Israelite religion was to be found in the official temples of the kingdom of Israel, not among a certain group in Judah and Jerusalem. In this connection we should note that S.M. Paul and W.G. Dever have maintained that Jeroboam's bulls 'were meant to be a popular cult' (*Biblical Archaeology*, p. 270). There is no support for such a statement. None of the bulls have been found, either in situ or anywhere else. If a bull statuette should be found at a nonofficial cult place one could draw a conclusion like that of Paul and Dever. However, Jeroboam was a king who had to reorganize the state religion and the state administration of Israel after the split with Jerusalem. Whatever he did in

Jerusalemite 'historiographers', the idea of the bull being a symbol for Yahweh has easily been associated with Baal. Bull figurines found in excavations from the territories of the Northern Kingdom cannot *a priori* be interpreted as representing Baal only.[1]

Reconstructing the history of the monarchies of Israel and Judah is problematic. The outlook of the textual material is clearly Jerusalemite and late. In character it is hostile toward the people of the former kingdom of Israel, which may be the audience for these writings about the Northern Kingdom.[2] The explanation for this may be sought in the hostility to the people of the North who seceded from Judah and its Davidic dynasty. This also explains the emphasis on David as the 'divinely' chosen one. This is not all, however. The books of Kings 'systematically' denounce both the Northern and the Southern Kingdoms for their 'sinfulness' and for not having followed the voice of the prophets. This is the explanation given for the destruction of these two kingdoms.[3] When history is depicted in such a programmatic way the historiography cannot be very reliable. We can also conclude that such a history is written in retrospect from a period when the people of the North made demands about being Yahweh's people too.

In trying to reconstruct the earliest periods of the peoples of Israel and Judah we have no reliable textual sources because the writers did

religious matters pertained to the official cult of the nation. What the deuteronomistic historian disliked does not equal popular religion.

1. A cult stand from Ta'anak, probably from the 10th cent. BCE, shows in the bottom register a naked woman and in the upper, fourth register a bull with a sundisk. Ruth Hestrin sees these as representing Baal and Asherah ('The Cult Stand from Ta'anach and its Religious Background', in *Studia Phoenicia*. V. *Phoenicia and the East Mediterranean in the First Millennium B.C.* [ed. E. Lipiński; Orientalia Lovaniensia Analecta, 22; Leuven: Peeters, 1987], pp. 61-77). The sundisk would rather indicate El, who perhaps had already been identified with Yahweh at Ta'anak.

2. Before one 'attempts to evaluate critically the significance of any work or to use it for historical purposes, one must investigate the readership or audience for which it was intended, the aims of the author', and why he organized his material as he did (E. Gabba, 'Literature', in *Sources for Ancient History* (ed. M. Crawford), p. 75.

3. G. Savran states that 'Kings marches steadily toward the terrible fate of the Northern Kingdom, then of the kingdom of Judah. This is a work which emphasizes the inexorability of that fate by its use of repetitive, stereotypical language and by a continuous demonstration of the reliability of prophecy' ('1 and 2 Kings', p. 147).

not know anything about the Bronze Age periods. Egyptian campaigns through Palestine were completely unknown to the biblical writers;[1] since these campaigns were recorded on pharaonic monuments that were not accessible to the biblical 'historiographers'. We should note that they did not know any Pharaoh by name before Shoshenq I. He was the first one who had become part of their history by his military exploits in Palestine. While mentions of Shoshenq's activity have been presented in Egyptian inscriptions as well as in the biblical account, the two accounts cannot be harmonized. The former[2] does not mention any siege of Jerusalem nor that its king, Rehoboam, paid tribute to the pharaoh. In the biblical presentation of Shoshenq's activity, on the other hand, the campaign is only associated with Rehoboam and Jerusalem. Nothing is mentioned about other parts of the country. Jeroboam's Israel does not even come into the picture. B. Halpern's assertion that Shoshenq's list can be used as a 'memoralization' 'of and proof for the Egyptian army having marched on Jerusalem and for Rehoboam having capitulated (1 Kgs 14.25-28; 2 Chron. 12.9-10) must accordingly be rejected.[3]

Biblical historiography is not a product built on facts.[4] It reflects the narrator's outlook and ideology rather than known facts.[5] As A.J. Huizinga has expressed it, 'every civilization creates its own form of history'.[6] Most of the writings about the premonarchic time are of

1.   See also D.B. Redford, 'An Egyptological Perspective on the Exodus Narrative', in *Egypt, Israel, Sinai. Archaeological and Historical Relationships in the Biblical Period* (ed. A.S. Rainey; Tel Aviv: Tel Aviv University, 1987), p. 138.

2.   H.H. Nelson (ed.), *Reliefs and Inscriptions at Karnak*. III. *The Bubastide Portal* (OIP, 74; Chicago: University of Chicago Press, 1954); J. Simons, *Handbook for the Study of Egyptian Topographical Lists Relating to Western Asia* (Leiden: Brill, 1937), pp. 89-101; W. Helck, *Die Beziehungen Ägyptens zu Vorderasien im 3. und 2. Jahrtausend v.Chr.* (2nd edn; Wiesbaden: Otto Harrassowitz, 1971), pp. 167-69.

3.   *The First Historians: The Hebrew Bible and History* (New York: Harper & Row, 1988), pp. 207-208.

4.   M. Liverani, 'Le "origini" d'Israele progetto irrealizzabile di ricerca etnogenetica', *Rivista Biblica Italiana* 28 (1980), pp. 15-16.

5.   The ideology may have been representative of a certain group.

6.   J. Huizinga, 'A Definition of the Concept of History', in *Philosophy and History: Essays Presented to Ernst Cassirer* (ed. R. Klibansky and H.J. Paton; New York: Harper & Row, 1936), pp. 7-8; see also Liverani, 'Le "Origini" d'Israele', pp. 9-32.

dubious historical value. Concerning the history of the early monarchic period, we have to realize that most people who became subjects of the new kingdom established in the central hills by Saul and then re-established by David were descendants of different clans and groups that had settled in the almost depopulated highlands during the 12th and 11th centuries BCE. They had come from different areas and backgrounds, some even from the north or from the east and southeast of Canaan.[1] It is doubtful that they could have had any knowledge of or traditions about events in the hills during the LB II period. F. Braudel's 'social history' or social time cannot, therefore, be demonstrated for the central hills during the LB period except at the few sites that had existed, such as at Shechem, Bethel and Jerusalem.[2] However, most of the settlers were indigenous to the land, which can be demonstrated by their material culture.[3] These groups of people could not have produced any historiography of common experiences before they had melded together and 'created' an ethnicity and had had a common history. Their common experience would have been recorded in official annals or administrative lists, which the biblical writer could then have 'extended' to all inhabitants of a region or a country.

For the origin of the territorial nation Israel we have only the biblical presentation referring to the conflict between Samuel and Saul that introduces the emergence of Saul's kingdom. Yet the account of the beginning of the monarchy is given in the style of a fairy-tale involving some asses, a prophet ruler, and a young man who found kingship instead of the asses he was looking for (a narrative in good Hans Christian Andersen style). The archaeological material of this period (c. 1015–980 BCE) does not provide any firm evidence for the existence of a monarchy in the hills. Neither are there any extrabiblical

---

1. See my article 'The Bull Figurine from Dhahrat et-Tawileh", *BASOR* 280 (1990), pp. 77-82.

2. We cannot, however, exclude the possibility of some nomads now and then 'inhabiting' parts of the area, but their 'social time' cannot be described or analyzed because of lack of source material.

3. G.W. Ahlström, *Who Were the Israelites?* (Winona Lake, IN: Eisenbrauns, 1986), pp. 11-36; I. Finkelstein, *The Archaeology of the Israelite Settlement* (Jerusalem: Israel Exploration Society, 1988). See also N.P. Lemche, *Early Israel. Anthropological and Historical Studies on the Israelite Society before the Monarchy* (VTSup, 37; Leiden: Brill, 1985).

literary sources to rely upon. Still, one usually considers Saul's kingdom to be factual. The question to be raised then is the following: is there any indication, textual or archaeological, that can be used for the existence of Saul's kingdom? The answer is yes. There is indirect textual indication in the fact that the biblical writers very strongly advocate that David, the usurper, was the chosen one. A mistake had been made. Ideologically, this is expressed by saying that Saul must have 'sinned'. In this way the mistake was 'corrected'. If Saul had been an insignificant ruler or even a nonexistent person, the biblical writer would not have gone to all the trouble of declaring that he fell out of divine grace and had to be replaced. Here, then, the historian can deduce that the biblical narrator had had a real problem in explaining the existence of a ruler who disturbed his ideological view. Because Saul had been an important king, the builder of the territorial state of Israel, his memory could not be erased, as was done in Egypt, for example. He could not be ignored. What one could do, though, was to paint his portrait with such negative colors that modern scholars are still inspired to declare him mentally sick.

Monumental buildings and fortifications bespeak 'most directly the might of the ruler', as A.L. Oppenheim expresses it; thus such activities can be seen as a government's political tools.[1] However, lacking textual information about these activities of the 11th century BCE we could ask the question: what government? Saul could have had rivals that the narrator did not mention.

We do not have any archaeological remains that we know of which can be associated with Saul. Neither is there any textual evidence for Saul having carried out a building program. The biblical narrator was not interested in such an aspect in connection with Saul. However, some building activity can be dated to the 11th century BCE. The settlement at Khirbet ed-Duwwara (coord. 141.5–177.8) 2.5 km southeast of Michmash at the Wâdi Suwenit has been dated to the late Iron I period. It is a small fortified site controlling the access to the Jordan Valley. It lasted for a short time only and may have been abandoned during the later part of the 10th century BCE.[2] The fact

---

1.   A.L. Oppenheim, 'Neo-Assyrian and Neo-Babylonian Empires', in *Propaganda and Communication in World History*, I, p. 113. See also Ahlström, *Royal Administration*, pp. 10-25, 70.

2.   Finkelstein, *Archaeology*, p. 64; *idem*, 'Kh. e-Duwwara", IEJ 38 (1988),

that a site under five dunams was fortified and surrounded by a 2–3 m wide wall may indicate that it served as a military outpost. That does not in itself mean that Saul or Samuel must have been the builder, even if both of them would be probable candidates. The archaeological material is not conclusive.

The identification of Tell el-Fûl with 'Saul's Gibeah' is problematic.[1] It has not been based on the archaeological remains but on conclusions drawn from biblical historiography.[2] The fortress ascribed to King Saul should probably be dated to a 'later phase of the Iron Age'.[3]

The skepticism one may have about the existence of the kingdom of David and Solomon might be justified since there are no corroborative nonbiblical texts mentioning these kings or their kingdom. The stories and all the episdoes about these two kings could be seen as fine literary products, somewhat reminiscent of a Shakespearean drama. It must be emphasized that the books of Samuel and Kings are not reports of historical events; rather, they are to be compared with historical novels. Still, it would be too easy to declare, as G. Garbini does, that the Davidic–Solomonic kingdom never existed on the basis that there are no inscriptional traces of any of the early kings of Israel and Judah.[4] This would be the same as saying that there were no kingdoms of Hamath, Ammon or Moab prior to their mention in inscriptions that happen to have been found. Even if Garbini is right in saying that no inscriptions have been found from the kings of Israel and Judah (before the Siloam inscription), this fact does not *per se* disprove the existence of an Israelite or a Judahite kingdom before the time of Hezekiah. We cannot completely disregard the biblical information about the Davidic–Solomonic kingdom, even if it is not contemporary with the artifacts that can be dated to this period. States have always needed propaganda to rule their territory by divine command, and this propaganda may have been kept alive through generations, espe-

pp. 79-80; see now also 'Excavations at Khirbet ed-Dawwara: An Iron Age Site Northeast of Jerusalem', *Tel Aviv* 17 (1990), pp. 163-208.

1. See J.M. Miller, 'Gibeah of Benjamin', *VT* 25 (1975), pp. 145-66.
2. W.F. Albright, *Excavations and Results at Tell el-Fûl (Gibeah of Saul)* (AASOR, 4; New Haven: American Schools of Oriental Research, 1924).
3. Finkelstein, *Archaeology*, p. 60.
4. G. Garbini, *History and Ideology in Ancient Israel* (trans. J. Bowden; New York: Crossroad, 1988), p. 17.

cially in such a case as that of David, the usurper. It should be self-evident that the textual depiction of the era of the 'United Monarchy' is by nature biased and at times fictional.[1] A harmonization of the textual material with the archaeological remains will in this case be problematic.

We are not allowed to conclude that a kingdom ruled by David and Solomon did not exist because no buildings or monuments have been found that explicitly name them as royal patrons. Neither can we dismiss the existence of their states because neither they nor their countries have been mentioned in any known, contemporary, non-biblical texts from the Near East. Around 1000 BCE, the Near Eastern political arena had lost its main powers, the empires of Anatolia, Mesopotamia and Egypt. The upheavals around 1200 BCE had eliminated the old power structure with its international contacts. Because no superpowers existed, there was no correspondence between them to have survived to be discovered. As we know, the Hittite kingdom collapsed, never to rise again. Assyria's power was at a low point at this time, so that no contact between its rulers and Palestine would have occurred. During the XXIst Dynasty Egypt had internal troubles stemming from the rivalry between Thebes and Tanis,[2] so any contact with, or interest in, a new Palestinian kingdom cannot be expected to have occurred or to have been recorded. Considering these facts, a kingdom of Israel could have existed; Egyptians and Assyrians had other problems to attend to.

Archaeologically, Palestine saw an increase in building activities during the 10th century BCE. The fortified 'cities' at Hazor, Megiddo and Gezer[3] with their almost identical gates[4] were not built by private

---

1.   The story about the conflict between Saul and David can be compared with an Indo-European literary theme in which the reigning king is opposed by a warrior hero. This theme is, also present for instance, in the Behistun inscription (Bardiya versus Darius); see W.T.H. Jackson, *The Hero and the King: An Epic Theme* (New York: Columbia University Press, 1982).

2.   Consult K.A. Kitchen, *The Third Intermediate Period in Egypt (1100–650 B.C.)* (Warminster: Aris & Phillips, 1977), pp. 3-23.

3.   For the discussion about Gezer's defense in the 10th cent., see W.G. Dever, 'Gezer Revisited', *BA* 47 (1984), pp. 213-17 and I. Finkelstein, 'The Date of Gezer's Outer Wall', *Tel Aviv* 8 (1971), pp. 136-45.

4.   This type of gate has also been found at Ashdod, stratum IX, from the 11th cent. BCE, which could indicate a Philistine origin; cf. W.G. Dever, 'Monumental

initiative, neither were the casemate walls[1] or the 'palaces' of these and other cities. The fact that there was a small fortified area and almost no residential buildings at Hazor (only half of the tell was used) is an indication that Hazor was not a city but a citadel in a national defense system. Monumental buildings and store cities, such as Beer-Sheba with its 4 m thick city wall,[2] were also most probably built by a government.[3] The mention in 1 Kgs 9.15 of the erection of fortifications at Hazor, Megiddo and Gezer is supported by the archaeological finds. Still, the archaeological remains do not prove the existence of the United Monarchy. In principle, all these activities could point to the existence of one or more governments, and we need to be aware that the dating of some of the fortifications and buildings could be inaccurate.[4]

Architecture in Ancient Israel in the Period of the United Monarchy', in *Studies in the Period of David and Solomon and Other Essays* (ed. T. Ishida; Winona Lake, IN: Eisenbrauns, 1982), p. 290.

1. For the casemate walls of this period, see N. Lapp, 'Canaanite Walls in Palestine and the Late Iron II Casemate at Tell el-Fûl (Gibeah)', *BASOR* 223 (1976), pp. 25-27. Rebuildings of casemate walls in Iron II (10th–9th cent. BCE) have been detected at Shechem, Tell Qasîle, Beth-Shemesh and Tell Beit Mirsim, according to N.L. Lapp (*The Third Campaign at Tell el Fûl: The Excavations of 1964* [AASOR, 45; Cambridge, MA: American Schools of Oriental Research, 1981], p. 49). Consult also Dever, 'Monumental Architecture', pp. 269-306.

2. Y. Aharoni, *Beer-Sheba. I. Excavations at Tel Beer-Sheba 1969–1971 Seasons* (Givatayim-Ramat Gan: Tel Aviv University, Institute of Archaeology, 1973), pl. 87.

3. The same may be the case at Khirbet el-Asheq ('En Gev) on the eastern shore of Lake Chinneret where one found a solid wall in stratum V, but a casemate wall in the following stratum. The latter is of the same type of those of the 10th cent. BCE in Cisjordan. The excavators, B. Mazar, A. Biran, M. Dothan and I. Dunayevsky considered it to be part of building activities undertaken during the United Monarchy ('Ein Gev, Excavations in 1961', *IEJ* 14 [1964], p. 9). Because 'En Gev is located on the eastern shore of the lake, it could just as well have belonged to an Aramaean kingdom.

4. A well-known example is the so-called Solomonic stable complex at Megiddo that was assigned to Ahab and Jezebel by Y. Yadin (*Hazor: The Discovery*, p. 214, and *Hazor*, pp. 154-56. After a careful investigation of the stratigraphy, Diane L. Saltz, dates the first 'equestrian complex', building 1576, to the reign of Jeroboam I ('Greek Geometric Pottery in the East. The Chronological Implications' [dissertation, Harvard University, Cambridge, MA, 1978], pp. 436-39).

5. *Conclusion*

A presentation of the history and religion of Israel and Judah must take into consideration both artifacts and texts. Such an approach will, however, always create some problems of interpretation because of the difference in character of these sources. Biblical historiography never was meant to give a historically accurate picture about events and religious phenomena. The goal of the biblical writers was to express the divine will, as they understood it. The biblical stories present an intentionally 'wishful' and/or theological picture of past times. Archaeology, on the other hand, 'speaks its own language' and therefore cannot be used as an interpretive tool for the textual material. It presents its own history, a history that in itself is difficult to explicate. Concerning the early monarchy, there are no archaeological facts that indisputably tell us of its existence and history. However, it would be hard to deny its existence. Certain memories and records seem to have existed, which have been the inspiration for later literary activities in subsequent eras. The kingdom probably emerged during the period 1015–990 BCE, but its grandeur is exaggerated, just as Saul's importance is minimized. Scattered pieces of artifacts and building remains, such as houses and fortifications, indicate both a growing population in the hills and the existence of some government(s).[1] The material culture of the following centuries yields a different picture than the one presented by the biblical writers. They were mainly interested in evaluating kings and nations according to their own concept of Yahwism. Therefore, what scholars usually call 'normative Yahwism' cannot be seen as a phenomenon that was in existence during most of the monarchic period. The Bible's 'normative Yahwism' has to be seen as the end product of a long process that resulted in the selection of the biblical texts. Normative Yahwism is the goal of the biblical writers and not something that can be identified with the official religion of the states of Israel or Judah, steering their fate and destruction. In light of the nature of the biblical textual material, with its 'end product, normative Yahwism', the harmonization of archaeological finds with textual phenomena is an

1. As to the socioeconomic situation, see I. Finkelstein, 'The Emergence of the Monarchy in Israel: The Environmental and Socio-Economic Aspects', *JSOT* 44 (1989), pp. 43-74.

almost impossible task. Therefore, any history of the monarchic period will by nature be tentative.

INDEXES

INDEX OF BIBLICAL REFERENCES

OLD TESTAMENT

INDEX OF AUTHORS

JOURNAL FOR THE STUDY OF THE OLD TESTAMENT

Made in the USA
Lexington, KY
06 September 2012